# Flying for Fun

# Flying for Fun
## in the southern Marches

*by*

**Tony Hobbs**

**Logaston Press**

LOGASTON PRESS
Little Logaston Woonton Almeley
Herefordshire HR3 6QH
logastonpress.co.uk


Published 2007
Copyright © Tony Hobbs 2007
Copyright © illustrations as acknowledged, otherwise Tony Hobbs

ISBN 978 1904396 79 6


Typeset by Logaston Press
and printed in Great Britain by
Oaklands Book Services, Gloucestershire

# Contents

# Acknowledgments

Firstly I must thank all those instructors who kindly agreed to take me up, or in the case of parachuting, down, in their aircraft or flying machine. They were: Steve Jones (Sabre Air Sports), Edi Geczy (Welsh Airsports), Walter Baumann (Midland Gliding Club), Dennis Davies (Herefordshire Aero Club), Gareth Abbott (Tiger Helicopters), Chris Gilmore (The Parachute Centre), Ian Ashpole (Wye Valley Aviation), Tizi Hodson (Tiger Airways), and Neville Payne (Wye Valley Flyers).

Then I must accord thanks to several local institutions who all proved friendly and helpful rather than bureaucratic. They were: Worcester History Centre, Hereford Museum and Library, Leominster Library, Radnorshire Museum, Llandrindod Wells Library, Monmouth Museum and Gloucestershire Archives.

For photographs and postcards, I am indebted to the following: Derek Foxton, Tim Ward, Andrew Helme (Monmouth Museum), Will Adams (Radnorshire Museum), David Stevens (Hereford Museum), Simon Wilkinson (The Parachute Centre), Andy (Cam - ARA for Tiger Airways), Neville Payne (Wye Valley Flyers), Derrick Eckley and Robbie Robertson (Black Mountains Gliding Club), Ken Joel (Hereford Parachute Club), Richard Screen (Tiger Helicopters), Edi Geczy (Welsh Airsports), Ian Ashpole (Wye Valley Aviation), and Phil and Chris Matthews (Cotswold Aero Club).

Other individuals I am beholden to for their invaluable contributions are (in no particular order): John Boxall, Phil Eade, Colin Fitzmaurice, Brian Davies, Jim Smith, Dewi Edwards, David Johnstone, Michelle Hall, Brian Marsh, John Hunt, Gordon Faulkner, Gerry Jones, Brian Crockett, John Bally, Chris Ellis, Keith Mansell, Toby Neal, David Corbett, Gay Baldwin, Brian Hales, Louise Ashpole, Barry Freeman, Alan Ramsden and Chris Rollings. If I have left anyone out, please put it down to forgetfulness on my part.

Among the books I consulted (please see the bibliography for full list), the most useful was *Wings over the Wye* whose author, Philip Hughes, was tragically killed in a crash soon after its publication in 1984. Lastly, I must thank Andy Johnson of Logaston Press for priming

# Introduction

'You're not doing a Jilly Cooper are you?' the receptionist at Gloucestershire Airport said when I told her I was writing a book called *Flying for Fun*.

'Certainly not,' I said. 'It's supposed to be serious.'

Another person queried: 'If you're not a flyer yourself, how come you're writing a book about flying?'

So my book, I'm afraid, contains no canoodling at 3,000ft, nor does it describe the enthralling experiences and technical know-how of a seasoned pilot.

What I have done, however, is to take a look at all the different forms of flying, from light aircraft and helicopters to microlights and paragliders, and from gliding and hot air balloons to parachuting, that are available in the southern Marches, together with details of where you can go to undertake these activities and how much it will cost. You will also find historical details of the fascinating early days of flying in the region, and how those weird machines evolved into today's streamlined craft. Several local aviators talk about their own experiences to bring the story up to date and bring a lively zest to the narrative.

I had, too, to find out for myself what it was like to undertake all these different flying activities, with, of course, the help of a qualified instructor. I wanted to taste the beauty, space and freedom of a new dimension, set the adrenaline flowing and test my nerve. And I wanted to show, too, that if I could do it, so could anyone irrespective of age and fitness, within reason that is.

Once you have experienced the sheer joy of flying, the freedom of the skies, and getting a different point of life, I am sure that you will become hooked and want to get back up there again. Or, if you prefer an armchair, maybe just to dream.

As Richard Bach, author of the famous book *Jonathan Livingstone Seagull*, said: 'There is a real Jonathan Seagull living within us all.'

Tony Hobbs
May, 2007

# Hot Air Balloons

Out of the clouds came a coach suspended from a monstrous ball in a kaleidoscope of colours. To the 40 odd harvesters in the corn field below, it was like some avenging angel or a chariot of fire. They all took to their heels, screaming and shouting. Except one old woman who stood stock still gazing in awe at this strange apparition from the heavens. Suddenly an anchor came tumbling down and then the face of a man appeared from the coach. 'Grab hold of the cord,' he bellowed, pointing to a dangling rope.

The year was 1785 and the place Stretton Grandison in Herefordshire. Nothing like this had ever been seen before — the first appearance over the southern Marches of a new phenomenon called a hot air balloon heralding man's first attempt at flying. It was made by the first Englishman to achieve the feat, on only his third ascent, and only two years after the world's first flight had been made in Paris.

The sole occupant, pioneer aeronaut James Sadler from Oxford, bellowed again and eventually managed to persuade the old woman to take hold of the cord. Curiosity no doubt getting the better of fear, the other harvesters returned to the scene and with their assistance the passenger basket, shaped like a coach, was brought to the ground followed by the balloon. It was indeed a colourful sight. The wicker basket was covered with purple silk, white festoons and gold trimmings, while the envelope, made from 500 yards of silk, was painted in pea green and yellow vertical stripes. It was filled with hydrogen rather than hot air. Afterwards Sadler travelled the three miles to Bromtrees Hall at Bishop's Frome, the home of Gilbert Nicholett, over which he had earlier flown and been invited to dinner at their hospitable table.

Sadler started life as a pastry cook at his father's shop in Oxford and later became technician at the University's chemical laboratory. In 1782 he heard about the Montgolfier brothers, Joseph and Jacques, who had publicly launched the first ever hot air balloon in France and a year later had made the first ever passenger balloon carrying the first aeronauts, Pilatre de Rozier and the Marquis d'Arlandes, with an ascent from the centre of Paris. He was inspired to become the first Englishman to make a similar flight. He somehow acquired a Montgolfier balloon, and in 1784 made the historic flight in Oxford. After a further ascent in Manchester, he came to Worcester in 1785. The *Gloucester Journal* of 29 August of that year reported the event:

> ... about half after one Mr. Sadler ascended with his balloon, amidst the acclamations of a crowd of ladies and gentlemen, in Mr. Wheeler's garden [The Pitchcroft, Worcester]. The wind was high, the day cloudy; and the traveller made little progress till he threw out three bags of ballast; and then saluting the spectators with his hat, he took a rapid ascent above the clouds, and was lost to our sight in about four minutes. At 37 minutes past two he approached the earth again so nearly as to converse with the people in the fields, who told him he was over Burford, near Tenbury, 21 miles from Worcester.

The balloon then re-ascended, and in a few minutes was passing over Bromtrees Hall and on to Stretton Grandison. After spending the night with the Nicholetts at Bromtrees, Sadler returned to Worcester, 'where the populace took the horses from his carriage and drew him about the streets in triumph.'

After another four ascents Sadler gave up ballooning until 1810 when he took it up again giving demonstrations in various parts of the country. After Sadler's 1785 flight, the skies over the Marches were left in peace, apart from small un-manned balloons and passenger balloons, anchored to the ground, at carnivals. It was to take a hundred years before another manned flight, from Monmouth, was undertaken in the early 20th century. The flight was made by Charles Rolls, son of a wealthy British peer who raced automobiles and helped found the Aero Club — the precursor 'Royal' was added later — 'to develop the science of aerial investigation in all its forms and applications.' In

*A replica of a full scale balloon, built by Walter Pritchard at Hereford in 1887. Of 1,200cu ft. the balloon, complete with small wicker basket and tiny ballast sacks, is pictured on the river tow path in Hereford (Derek Foxton Collection)*

1904 he joined forces with car manufacturer Frederick Royce to form the household name of Rolls-Royce.

Some confusion surrounds the actual date that Rolls made the first ascent and in which balloon. According to Philip Hughes in *Wings over the Wye*, the flight was made on Easter Monday, 16 April 1906 in the 42,000 cubic feet balloon *Venus* before a crowd of almost 1,000 spectators at May Hill, Monmouth. The balloon, inflated by coal gas from the nearby gas works, was released and 'rapidly rose to an altitude of about 7,000ft before drifting majestically away in an easterly direction towards Ross-on-Wye and eventually Gloucestershire.'

However, the *Monmouthshire Beacon* of 20 April 1906 reports that on that Easter Monday it was a balloon called *Dolce Far Niente*, of 45,000 cubic feet, which made the ascent at Monmouth. There is no mention of it being the inaugural flight.

It seems likely, therefore, that the first flight was made a year or two earlier, but in which balloon is still not clear. And, according to records at the Monmouth Museum, the earliest *Beacon* report (30 September 1904) of hot air balloons at Monmouth is of a balloon chase by motor car from Birmingham to Rolls' home at The Hendre, near Monmouth.

Returning to the *Beacon* report of 1906, Rolls was accompanied in the *Dolce Far Niente*, by Frank Butler, owner of the balloon, Professor A.K. Huntington, a member of the Aero Club, and John Holder, of

Worcester. Summer-like weather on Easter Monday 'attracted hundreds of spectators to May Hill where Mr. J. Hall kindly lent his field, facing the Gas Works, and a six-inch main was used for the purpose of inflating

*At end of the 1800s, this balloon is preparing to take off in Ross in what was then a field in Smallbrook road alongside the Gloucester Road (in which the spectators are standing). (Fred Druce)*

the balloon. ... Excited helpers were at last given the warning to "let go," and with cheers and waving of caps and handkerchiefs, the balloon soared gracefully away... ere long the immense balloon was a tiny speck, six thousand feet above, and moving in the direction of the Forest of Dean.'

After lunch over Symonds Yat, the *Dolce Far Niente*, flew over Newnham and finally came down on a farm at Upton St. Leonards, near Gloucester. The ascent was controlled by dumping ballast bags of fine sifted sand, and descent by valving the gas.

*J.T.C. Moore-Brabazon, Professor Huntington and Charles Rolls (left to right) pictured at a Balloon meet, Whitsuntide 1907, at Winchester gasworks (Monmouth Museum)*

The meadow became a regular launching site for balloon ascents, many of which were of a competitive nature, taking place every Easter and Christmas for the next three years. One of these was named the 'Hare and Hounds', for which Rolls offered a prize, where the hound balloons had to chase a hare balloon across country. Rolls was usually the 'hare' in a light balloon of his own called *Imp*, which he transported on his specially equipped Silver Ghost. Another test of aerial skill was a flight from London with the intention of landing within a twenty-mile radius of The Hendre, the family home of Rolls' father, Baron Llangattock, who offered a prize to the balloon which landed the closest. Apart from a brush with railway trucks at one take-off in 1908 and the danger of the gasometer running out of gas, there were no mishaps. Rolls often took up with him a penny whistle with which he treated his companions 'to the tunes of England and Scotland and the enchanting airs of the London halls.'

Rolls built up a fleet of balloons, including the 17,500cu ft *Midget*, and the *Imp*, of 11,000cu ft, both of which he flew from Monmouth. But he had also seen the practical limitations of ballooning, describing it

*The* Imp *stowed away in the back of Charles Rolls' specially equipped Silver Ghost. (Monmouth Museum)*

*Mrs Havard's balloon which Rolls borrowed and was piloting with his mother as a passenger on Boxing Day 1908, pictured in front of the family home, The Hendre (Monmouth Museum)*

*Monsieur Dollfus' balloon near the Vron, New Radnor during the French Aero Club's balloon race in 1914. A policeman guards the basket (W.H. McKaig)*

as 'essentially a sport pure and simple,' and after some 160 flights turned his attention to the question of heavier than air flight. During the course of his travels all over Europe and the United States, he met the Wright brothers, who had made the first powered flight in 1903. Rolls bought an experimental Wright Flyer biplane, which he flew in 1910 from Dover across the Channel and back on the first non-stop return flight. A few weeks later, he was killed when his biplane crashed at a flying display near Bournemouth.

On the eve of his death, Rolls said: 'There are more ways of flying than dying ... I have given all my life to it — all my life ... We all give our lives to something — give them away.' At the age of 33, he was Britain's first aircraft fatality. A statue in Monmouth town square shows Rolls examining a model of the Wright Flyer in which he lost his life.

Without the support of Rolls, ballooning in Monmouth came to an end as shortly afterwards, with the outbreak of the First World War, did the days of fashionable sporting pastimes. In any case there was far more interest now in the potential of fixed wing aircraft. As far as hot air balloons in this region was concerned, another 70 years was to lapse before the next milestone was reached with the establishment of Wye Valley Aviation, based at Ross-on-Wye.

Set up in 1980 by Ian Ashpole, the company offers hot air balloon flights over the Wye Valley from several sites in Ross and Hereford and also teaches people to gain their Balloon Pilot's Licence. Ian first became interested in the sport after interviewing a balloonist while working as a journalist on the *Ilford Recorder*. He then joined Colin Prescot at his Hot Air Balloon Company in Surrey, later styled Flying Pictures, for which he became chief pilot. He is also a parachutist and holds a private pilot's licence. According to the 1999 edition of the Guinness Book of World Records, the company has 'planned and executed air stunts for more than 200 feature films and coordinated the aerial stunts for hundreds of TV shows and ads.'

While with Flying Pictures Ian flew balloons and carried out stunts at the UK air display circuit including the Royal Show, Three Counties and Bath & West and ran balloon events in the United States. During 25 years of global travel he has flown balloons in 28 different countries including New Zealand (eight tours), Australia, Russia, the United States, Nepal, and on the Continent and in South America. He has also set a number of records for hot air balloon stunts, many performed over Ross-on-Wye, with TV coverage including the 'And Finally' spot on ITV News.

Ian's first world record attempt was in 1986 on the highest-ever trapeze act for David Frost's Guinness Book of Records, which he accomplished in a balloon sponsored by Alka-Seltzer, at a height of 16,400ft over Cambridge. For this feat he used an oxygen canister and mask which malfunctioned and he only just made it back into the basket, suffering from hypoxia.

Three years later he went after the record for the highest bungee jump by leaping out of a balloon, bouncing up and down on the elastic strapped to his ankles and

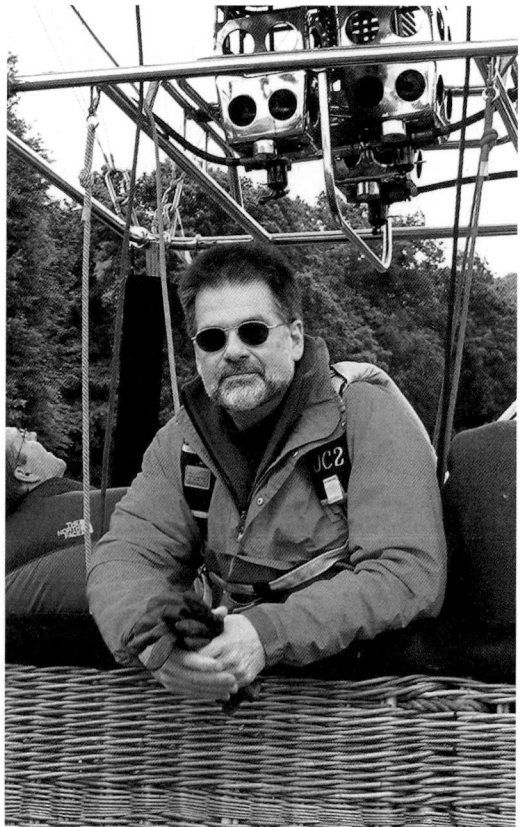

*Ian Ashpole. (Ian Ashpole)*

then cut himself loose before parachuting down. The rehearsal was staged over Ross-on-Wye as an exclusive for the Sunday newspaper, the *People*. In his book *To the Edge of Space*, Colin Prescot said: 'It worked fine except that there was a design fault in the bungee release mechanism. However much he struggled he couldn't get free'. He screamed up at the balloon pilot that he would have to land with him still suspended from the balloon. Still dangling upside down, Ian swung gently by a farmhouse. 'Is it all right if I land here?', he asked the astonished farmer and his wife who were sitting up in bed. Moments later he was a heap on the ground. Undaunted, Ian fixed the release mechanism and a few days later set off for the real thing. The balloon climbed to 16,000ft and he successfully jumped, the result appearing on national TV bulletins.

Another stunt over Ross-on-Wye took place in 1993 when he achieved the world's highest tightrope walk performed between two balloons, sponsored by Citroen and Champagne Mercier at over 11,000ft. The only concessions to safety were to use an iron bar instead of a rope and wearing a parachute under his overalls.

But the stunt that Ian thinks was probably the best involved being carried beneath 600 toy balloons filled with helium in 1997. With some of the balloons bursting like automatic gun fire on the way up, he climbed to over 10,000ft before cutting the balloons adrift with a knife and then parachuting back down to land. This gained him an additional entry in the Guinness Book of Records.

Two other stunts both involved flights from Ross-on-Wye in connection with the Bristol Balloon Fiesta. The first, in 1998, had Ian actually standing on top of the crown of a balloon while it was high in the sky. The second, a year later, had him taking it easy at 6,000ft in a hammock suspended between two balloons as pre-publicity for Sainsbury's Flying Circus. After enjoying a 30-minute ride in the hammock, Ian skydived to the ground.

All in all, Ian has clocked up 2,500 hours flying hot air balloons, 580 hours gas and hot air airships, 800 hours fixed wing aircraft, 50 hours microlight and undertaken 1,200 jumps as a free fall parachutist. In recognition of his services in the field of balloon stunts, Ian was presented with the Royal Aero Club silver medal by Prince Andrew a few years ago. Charles Rolls would no doubt have approved.

'It's the flying that appeals to me,' he said. 'I just like being in the air, flying a kite even. Balloons just happened to be first after model aircraft.

They are simple, easy, uncomplicated, very sound, safe and robust. No two flights are the same. We tend to fly at sunset or evening and see the world at its best.'

When Ian was away on his travels, Wye Valley Aviation was looked after by other pilots, but a few years ago he left Flying Pictures to concentrate on his own business. Flights vary from two to four passengers in the VIP balloons to a group of up to eight in the larger balloon. Flights, which cost from £145 per person with reductions for group bookings, last about one hour over a distance from between five and 15 miles though the total time is about three to four hours. After landing the flight is celebrated with Champagne before returning to the take-off site. Flights are spread all the year round and take off from various sites in the Ross and Hereford area. Chief flying instructor is Rob Little, a commercial pilot, while the operations director is Ian's wife, Louise, who looks after administration and crews.

*Above and opposite: two views of Ian Ashpole's 1997 exploit of being carried by 600 toy balloons filled with helium which earned him an entry in the Guinness Book of Records for the world's highest flight by man using toy balloons. The pictures also show the range in balloons that now take to the skies. (Ian Ashpole)*

Also available is a course for people who wish to obtain their private pilot's licence (balloons). There is a minimum of 18 hours instruction and five written examinations, a total of about 25 hours spread over 12 months. The cost is up to £5,000. And for those who pass and want to fly on their own, second hand balloons, all thoroughly checked and with MOT certificates, can be obtained for between £3,500 and £5,000.

Among other facilities provided are event management, aerial advertising, air charter and aerial imaging.

When it came to my turn to go up in one of Ian's hot air balloons I had a long wait for the weather to improve. Then one perfect summer morning I received a call from Louise. 'Can you make it this evening?' she asked. I certainly could. 'See you at the Chase Hotel in Ross at 7.30 tonight then.' But when I got there, had I arrived at the right place? The grounds of the Chase were full of young people, all looking very smart and elegant in evening dress, while the car park was full of unusual vehicles: a pink stretch limousine, an American Jeep, an old fire engine, with the words Party Pump, and a grey double decker bus with Plastic in bold letters, to name a few. Then a young man arrived on a tricycle covered in balloons.

Was this the launching site for my first ride in a hot air balloon? I was heartened by the arrival of a Land Cruiser and trailer on which stood a

wicker basket and burners, with Ian and Louise in attendance. We were joined by two other passengers, John and Hilary Guyver, also on their first ever trip.

Apparently the young folk had come for a sixth form leaving party with disco and dancing. Of more concern was the news that two helicopters were arriving bringing more students, no doubt trying to outdo their comrades in mode of transport. No sooner had Ian released a toy balloon filled with helium, which shot upwards heading towards Gloucester, for a final wind check than the first helicopter arrived, disgorging revellers onto the lawns. Deciding that the present situation was a little on the busy side, Ian ordered us into the Cruiser and after a skirmish with the tangle of vehicles drove through Ross towards the bypass, turning off onto a grassy patch by the river Wye.

Then Ian and his crew, Louise and Rob Little, started to make ready the balloon in an intricate but well rehearsed routine. First the balloon was manhandled off the trailer and then the basket. Taken out of its container, the balloon was unrolled along the grass for seemingly yards and yards and then a machine was set up which began pumping in cold air. The balloon enlarged and then blossomed into all its glory up into

*Preparing Ian Ashpole's balloon for my flight. Cold air is pumped in*

the air. The wicker basket had been attached and a unit of four burners connected to two tanks of gas. We were ready for lift-off. Ian, wearing safety belt and thick gloves, ushered us aboard, showed us the crouch position — in case of a heavy landing — and then turned on one of the burners. With a wave to some bystanders who had come to watch, we smoothly, majestically rose up into the still evening air, it was by now 8 o'clock, and 'up, up and away.' Soon the people below were just dots as we headed back and over Ross. The air was crystal clear and the town looked in pristine condition. The church and other landmarks like the Pavilion Hotel stood out bold and clear. Looking down as we rose higher, it now looked more like a model or toy town. Tiny people in gardens, tending barbecues, waved at us and, rather regally, we waved back. Except when Ian was blasting flames up into the balloon, it was so quiet, so peaceful. We crossed the Wye, our image reflected in the water, and headed towards Much Marcle. Ian explained that there was a spread of air currents which gave us various flying options. Just in case he carried a GPS. Our speed was about 7mph.

Slowly rising now to a height of about 2,000ft, the air became cooler with a faint breeze fanning our cheeks. Looking around we could make

*The balloon is almost filled*

*The burner in operation as the balloon lifts off*

out Slimbridge and the river Severn to our right, Sugar Mountain and Hay Bluff behind us and to our left the Malvern Hills, its switchback shape very clear. We could also make out Woolhope, where John and Hilary live, and the surrounding ridge which, according to Ian, was the lip of an ancient volcano. Fancy living near a volcano, I thought. Bare fields below showed precision ploughing marks and in grassy fields sheep looked like seeds of grain.

Flying lower now, we passed over the stately manor house formerly owned by Sir John Harvey Jones, of Trouble Shooter fame. The lovely gardens included three or four large ornamental pools. From a nearby house, bonfire smoke spumed upwards — another wind indicator.

'Let's take a look at the wildlife,' Ian said and down we swooped over fields of curly kale, a few bunnies breaking into a run at our approach, and up a bank, the bottom of the basket brushing the long grass tops.

'Impressive, it really is,' said Hilary. Some disturbed pheasants ran off noiselessly, equally impressed. Now Ian had to negotiate some telegraph wires; 'we've always got to be on the look out for wires,' he said.

Then over a lake, a swan proudly showing off her flock of no fewer than eight cygnets, and a few moorhens skidding around. Somewhere was the mewing sound of buzzards, but we didn't see them.

Ian informs us that he will attempt to bring us down on the car park of the South Hereford Golf Club, not far away. But first a hill full of trees is in the way. With remarkable dexterity, Ian gradually moves the balloon upwards with short bursts of flame and we rise slowly over the tree tops, caressing the top-most leaves. I plucked one and then let it flutter down to rejoin its comrades. Down the other side and over more long grass, sweet smelling, and a cock pheasant ambling away. Now we come to a corn field, the golf club on the further side, and with diminishing air Ian landed us gently on part of the field where the barley had been cut. We had unintentionally landed on private land. His two helpers had already arrived and were waiting on the road by the club.

'We'll try the sling-shot approach,' said Ian, as Rob and Louise approached. 'Throw him at the corn.' As we lifted slightly, they added their weight to the basket, and we drifted over the barley, the basket just tickling their seed-heads. But it was of no avail. The wind had died completely and we drifted back to the side and landed again on the corn

*The balloon reflected in the waters of the Wye*

stubs. After disembarking, we gave a hand with gathering the balloon, still puffing out hot air, into its container, rather like a genie returning to its bottle, and then manhandled it and the basket back onto the trailer. Amazing that this huge balloon had disappeared within minutes with nothing to remind us of our trip.

'What a fantastic experience,' said John, who had taken early retirement from Xerox, the document company at Mitcheldean, and was now celebrating his second wedding anniversary with Hilary. 'I'd certainly like to do it again, perhaps somewhere like the Serengeti safari park.'

'I had this weightless feeling, just drifting,' said Hilary. 'And the peacefulness.'

'I think this deserves some champagne,' said Ian, whipping out a bottle of bubbly from a picnic basket. And, standing in the stubble, we raised our glasses to Ian and his team and to hot air ballooning.

For my part, it was a memorable experience. Providing the conditions are good, there is no doubt that hot air ballooning is one of the best forms of air travel: sedate, relaxed, graceful, with silent speed, and affording unrestricted, beautiful views of sky and countryside. My only reservation would be perhaps the uncertainty of making a smooth landing. Or, as L.T.C. Rolt in his book *The Balloonists* more poetically puts it: 'Only the balloon, a frail bladder of gas, unguidable, beautiful, comical, tragically ephemeral, a spherical microcosm of the great globe itself, affords man an aerial platform upon which we may stand, staring down in silence upon the mystery of his turning world.'

# Light Aircraft

Watched by only a handful of people on a lonely stretch of land near Kitty Hawk in North Carolina on 17 December 1903, brothers Orville and Wilbur Wright created history. Their biplane, the Wright Flyer, became the first powered, heavier-than-air machine to achieve a controlled and sustained flight with a pilot aboard. The aircraft, built of sticks and fabric and powered by an internal combustion engine, was airborne for only 12 seconds, but after three more attempts that same day it flew for about a minute and covered a distance of 250 metres. At the time very little interest was shown in these events. But the world of flying, previously the preserve of hot air balloons, would never be the same again.

It was to be another five years before Britain's first flight was achieved by the hugely colourful Samuel Franklin Cody, otherwise known as the Flying Cowboy. Cody was born Franklin Cowdery in the United States, where he was cowboy, frontiersman, showman and playwright. At some point he changed his name to Cody after the famous cowboy showman Buffalo Bill.

Cody came to Britain in 1896, later becoming naturalised, and continued his interest in man-lifting kites, giving demonstrations to the Royal Navy and Army, who employed him as Chief Kiting Instructor at the Balloon School in Farnborough. He developed glider kites, fitted them with engines, and progressed to powered aircraft. In a contraption of wood, metal and fabric with a 50 horsepower French engine, he flew a distance of about a quarter of a mile on 16 October 1908 to record the first official sustained British flight. With the performance of aircraft quickly improving, Cody took part in round-Britain races in 1910 and 1911 and was photographed with his plane in Pitchcroft, Worcester in August of that year. Cody, who also helped design the first British airship,

17

*'Col. Cody with his aeroplane on Pitchcroft', from Berrow's* Worcester Journal,
*12 August 1911*

was awarded the silver medal by the Aeronautical Society. He died in 1913 when the seaplane he was flying broke in half; he was buried with full military honours.

However, although there is no mention of him in any of the official history books, another claimant for the title of Britain's first aviator has recently emerged, that of Ernest Maund from Craven Arms, Shropshire. Like the Wright brothers, who had run a bicycle shop and made bicycles before their interest became focussed on aeroplanes, Ernest also made cycles and owned a garage and cycle shop in Craven Arms. He too became interested in flying and started to make his own flying machines. Faded photographs dated 1907 show Ernest standing proudly in front of his aircraft and another in the cockpit. A sign on the plane reads 'Briton No. 1.' His eldest son, Fred, who died in 1983, recorded that Ernest '... built his aeroplane and completed it in January 1907. ... He took it to a field at Stokesay, it went to about house-top height and crashed. Engine was under-powered, could not lift his weight.'

*Ernest Maund. (Maund family)*

Fuelling the intrigue is a ticket, with the date 1907 on the back,

18

*Ernest Maund is pictured in the pilot's seat with brother Percy behind and his wife, Alice, on the right. The lady on the left is believed to be Percy's wife, Edie.*
*(Maund family)*

which reads: 'Craven Arms Aero Cub. This ticket entitles the holder to admission to the ground on the day of flight, which will be advertised in local paper. Price 1s. ...' This makes the family believe that Maund must have given flying exhibitions.

Coming out heavily on the side of Ernest Maund is aviation historian Mike Grant who, in his book *Wings Across the Border – a History of Aviation in North Wales and the Northern Marches*, writes: 'Without a doubt, he [Maund] was the first British national to fly.' Grant added that in three months Maund built a monoplane which he flew from a field at nearby Stokesay on 14 July 1904, just a few months after the Wright brothers' first flight and four years before Cody's. 'On one run he achieved a height of 40ft and length of 400ft, before fuel starvation brought him to the ground.' He has no idea why Maund's achievement has been overlooked. The date 1904, however, seems too early to be credible. Until further concrete evidence is forthcoming, the jury is still out as to whether or not Ernest Maund is deserving of a place in history. But it would be nice to

*Ernest Maund stands by his plane in 1907. (Maund family)*

think that he had upstaged the flamboyant Flying Cowboy. As a matter of interest, Maund invented the first dipping head-lamp for cars and fathered no fewer than 19 children!

Another early plane maker was William Butcher, who ran the first motor garage in Ross-on-Wye. The first indication of his interest in flying was an advert which appeared in the *Ross Gazette* dated 7 October 1909. It read: 'Aeroplane work — wanted, a smart lad. Must be clever at light wood-work. G & W Butcher, the Motor House, Ross.' Another advert followed (see right), on 18 November, which, under a picture of a primitive flying machine, declared: 'Aviation in Ross — A Full Size Aeroplane is now in course of construction by G and W Butcher. If interested, watch its progress.' Then followed details of scale model aeroplanes for sale.

# Aviation in Ross

## A FULL SIZE AEROPLANE

Is now in course of construction by G. and W. BUTCHER, of The Motor House, Brookend-street, Ross.

IF INTERESTED, WATCH ITS PROGRESS.

## MODEL FLYING,

For study and experiment by amateurs, and as the most educational mechanical toy for boys, we carry stock of the splendid

## "FINBAT" SCALE MODEL AEROPLANES.

CODY, WRIGHT, BLERIOT, LATHAM, CURTISS, AND FARMAN TYPES.

Largest range and most perfectly constructed models in the world. From **12/6** to **£2 2s.**

Also a great variety of spare parts. Write for fully illustrated priced list. B.G

## G. & W. BUTCHER,
AEROPLANE DEPT., THE MOTOR HOUSE, and 24, 25, and 26, Brookend-street, ROSS.

20

*The Butcher brothers' aircraft. Around 1910, early one Sunday morning they pushed their craft out of its shed on Brookend. Four helpers mounted on bicycles, held on to the wings and tail, and pedalled up to a field above the Kerne Bridge. Unfortunately their attempt to take off proved fruitless.*
*(Derek Foxton Collection)*

The following year, Mr. Butcher and fellow enthusiasts managed to build an aeroplane from a design contained in the newly founded *Flight* magazine. It looked like a tricycle with an engine at the back and a propeller in front. On top were two cumbersome wings with wooden slats in between. It was taken to a field five miles out of Ross high above Kerne Bridge on the Bishopswood Estate for a trial flight.

'Sadly though success was not to be theirs,' wrote Fred Druce in his book *A good plain country town - Ross-on-Wye 1800-1930*, 'for, after their machine had raced madly around the field and charged through several hedges without rising an inch, it was reluctantly agreed by all present that for the time being at least they were going to remain firmly earth bound.' Later the engine and propeller were stripped from their mountings and lashed to a rowing boat which they then used to roar up and down the river.

Worthy of mention is another Ross inhabitant, Mr. C.H. Parkes, who also experimented with aeroplanes. According to the *Ross Gazette* of 14 October 1909, Mr. Parkes achieved some measure of success with biplanes as illustrated in *Flight*. 'The earlier machine shown was mounted upon an ordinary push bicycle, but the propeller was coupled with the pedals and the rear wheel disconnected from them. In this way he was

*This is believed to be the aircraft of William Butcher of Ross-on-Wye in about 1910, although it bears comparison with the description of C.H. Parkes' aircraft, also built in Ross. (Derek Foxton Collection)*

able by vigorous pedalling to obtain a speed of about 9mph on the flat, but the only occasions on which the machine left the ground at all were when endeavouring to start on a down grade, and then the length of jump was only a yard or two at longest.'

Mr. Parkes built an improved version with a 4hp air-cooled motor mounted above a light three-wheeled carriage just behind the pilot's seat. 'The entire machine, with Mr. Parkes on board, scaled about 850lbs complete, and with it some successful "jumps" of from 10 to 40ft were accomplished.'

The report added that Mr. Parkes 'is at the present time completing a monoplane from which he hopes to derive considerably greater satisfaction.'

Another great early builder of aircraft was the French engineer Louis Blériot, who was the first to fly across the Channel, from Calais to Dover in 37 minutes in 1909, in the monoplane he designed. He scooped a £1,000 prize offered by the *Daily Mail* for this achievement. Full scale production of the 50hp Blériot monoplane followed, one of which was the first aircraft to land in Herefordshire, on 17 April 1912, even though it was by accident.

The pilot, Mr. R. Corbett Wilson, was racing Mr. Damer Allen from London to Dublin to be the first to cross the Irish Sea, when he was forced to land in 'the big field at Newchurch' (near Almeley), according

*Three views of R. Corbett Wilson's plane in the field at Newchurch. (Tim Ward)*

to startled farmworkers when he asked where he was. He was having difficulty in finding his way to Chester, the agreed staging post, after dropping his compass out of the aircraft. After spending the night in Hereford, where he was joined by his French mechanic and buying a new compass, petrol and oil, Wilson set off again to a hearty send-off by a large crowd.

However, he only travelled a dozen miles before his Blériot developed engine trouble at 3,000ft and he had to make another unscheduled

*Preparing R. Corbett Wilson's plane at Newchurch for his continued flight (Hereford Museum) ... only to have to land again near Colva (below). (W.H. McKaig)*

stop, landing a few feet from a hedge at Colva in Radnorshire. It was to take another three days before he was able to take off again during which time his recalled mechanic sorted the engine and faulty oil pump. Though the hour was early in the morning, a large crowd from Kington and many miles around had congregated to watch his departure. Wilson flew on to Fishguard and the following day flew across the Irish sea and landed near Wexford. Unfortunately, Mr. Allen was lost with his plane in the Irish Sea.

A few months later Henri Salmet, chief flying instructor at the Hendon Blériot school, went on a tour of South Wales and the Midlands as part of a series of events around the country organised by the *Daily Mail*. Salmet, accompanied by a mobile ground crew including his wife, arrived in Cardiff early in July but was then promptly taken ill. His flight was delayed until 18 July when he took off for Ross-on-Wye, but his engine was misfiring and he made an unscheduled landing at Raglan. The Salmets motored on to Ross for dinner, returning to their aircraft the following day. Despite poor visibility, he took off and after giving a short display to the local crowds, flew on at heights of up to 5,000ft over the Monmouthshire hills to Ross, landing at Hildersley golf course. The next leg to Hereford had to be postponed but after another overnight

*Henri Salmet coming in to land at Ross (Hereford Journal)*

*Salmet dismounting from his plane at Hereford. The signature on the card is that of de Havilland, a name that was to become important as an aircraft manufacturer in the UK. It is not known if he was present at Hereford on this occasion, or happened to sign the postcard some time later. (Tim Ward)*

stop, Salmet took off the following afternoon and flying sometimes as low as 800ft above ground level in order to see the landmarks, he arrived at Hereford racecourse 15 minutes later. He made a perfect landing to the jubilation of the crowds and reminding one reporter 'of nothing so much as a huge dragon fly.'

Salmet immediately examined the 50hp Gnome engine, which had been misfiring, but after some adjustments and a short test flight he was able to greet his well-wishers. He then delighted the crowd, who had written their signatures on the plane's canvas coverings, with a display of

*Policemen hold on to Salmet's aircraft as he revs the engine prior to take off from Hereford. (Hereford Journal)*

*Taxiing commences at Ross*

aerobatic skills. With visibility still poor the onward flight to Worcester was delayed until after the weekend, with Sunday spent dining with the Mayor and visiting local gentry.

On Monday 22 July, Salmet took off for Worcester. Low clouds prevented him from even seeing the Malvern Hills and, fearful of running into a thunderstorm, he landed in a field at Broadheath, four miles from Worcester. A fishmonger was passing at the time on his bicycle and asked if he could be of any assistance. He couldn't and instead signed his name on the aeroplane. Salmet took off again and despite misty conditions eventually found the city and landed at Pitchcroft, the same site from which James Sadler had taken off in his balloon 127 years previously. Asked what his flight was like, Salmet replied: 'Oh, very bad, the weather was misty. I cannot see. What can I do in such weather?'

*Salmet's aircraft at Hereford racecourse. (Hereford Journal)*

27

The first aircraft to arrive in the southern Marches with a passenger on board was a Royal Flying Corps biplane which landed at Monmouth on 25 August 1912 after flying from Weymouth in a time of 65 minutes. The pilot was Lieut. Fox of the Royal Engineers with Lieut. Burchard Ashton as his passenger.

Another celebrated pilot of the time was Gustav Hamel, son of an English naturalised German doctor, who carried the first official air mail from London to Windsor in 1911. In the summer of 1912 he gave flying displays before large crowds at various locations in Shropshire. After making the first non-stop flight from Dover to Cologne in April 1913, Hamel visited Llandrindod Wells in August as the first pilot to land on the old racecourse which was later to become one of the first commercial airfields in the area. This 25-acre site adjoining the Rock Park Hotel was the enterprising idea of Tom Norton, owner of the Automobile Palace and pioneer in the cycle and motor business. Over 4,000 people paid to watch Hamel give three displays, in the second of which he was accompanied by a female passenger, Lady Victoria Perry, to reinforce his 'dashing' reputation. A local newspaper reported: 'Each display had its peculiar features. The bankings, vol-planes and pan-cake descents, and the fascinating turnings and evolutions were watched with the keenest possible interest.' So successful was the exhibition that Hamel made a return visit two weeks later when he again enthralled a huge crowd. But a year later Hamel was dead, his aircraft disappearing during a flight over the Channel.

*Gustav Hamel (on the right) standing in front of his plane. (Radnorshire Museum)*

*The Ddole airfield at Llandrindod Wells in the 1930s.*
*(Radnorshire Museum)*

Another famous aviator, Benjamin C. Hucks, the first British airman to follow the example of Hamel and loop a Blériot, visited Hereford on 3 and 4 September 1913. He signalled his arrival by flying round the cathedral tower and then over the cattle market, creating a 'hubbub' and interrupting business. People poured out of pubs and shops to catch a glimpse of the aircraft. Hucks then gave a flying exhibition at Bartonsham Meadow, watched by 3,000 fee-paying spectators and thousands more, for free, from the other side of the Wye. Despite the high charge of £5, many people took the opportunity the next day of enjoying for the first time short trips around the city. The first passenger, Mr. E. Arnold

*Hucks' Blériot aircraft at Bartonsham Meadows, Hereford on 3 September 1913.*
*(Derek Foxton Collection)*

*Hucks' aircraft preparing for take off on Bartonsham Meadows, the 'brakes' again being supplied by manpower holding onto the rear fuselage. (Derek Foxton Collection)*

Watkins, who had promoted the event, described flying 'as one of the most exciting and enjoyable experiences of my life.' Another passenger commented: 'My flight was the most delightful thing I have ever done. It was ripping.' It is said that Hucks only came to aviation after being banned from driving a car for three years for a speeding offence!

Tom Norton promoted another aerial exhibition at Llandrindod Wells in the summer of 1914 with a display by Vivian Hewitt. But soon

*Vivian Hewitt's plane on its car pulled trailer outside the Automobile Palace in Llandrindod Wells. (Radnorshire Museum)*

afterwards the First World War started and all civil flying over Britain was banned except within three miles of a recognised aerodrome. The ban was not removed until 1 May 1919.

After the war surplus military aircraft, particularly the Avro 504, were converted to take two passengers and used to give joy rides. For instance Captain Brettell offered daily flights from 17 to 22 July 1920 from Oldfield, Huntingdon, Hereford. With the cost of a flight slashed from £5 per person in 1913 to a guinea, these proved popular and also led to air taxi services being introduced. One such flight was made by Mr. Geoffrey Le Mander from Castle Bromwich to the Leominster Agricultural Show in September 1920. One air taxi/pleasure trip firm was South Wales Airways Ltd., which in 1927 were flying from Bridgend to Llandrindod Wells, where the Rock Park Hotel airfield was continuing to be used.

In 1929 great excitement greeted the news that the celebrated Sir Alan Cobham was to visit Hereford in his huge de Havilland 61 with room for ten passengers during his Youth of Britain tour. Cobham was no stranger to the area having spent time working on his cousin's farm at Brockbury Hall, Colwall, 16 years previously. But his destination lay elsewhere — in the exciting world of aviation. At the outbreak of the First World War he joined the Army Veterinary Corps but transferred to the Royal Flying Corps and became a flying instructor. In 1921 he joined the newly formed de Havilland Aeroplane Hire Service (slogan: 'Fly Anyone – Anywhere') and was soon making epic flights to India and South Africa and then, in 1926, flew a de Havilland 50 J seaplane all the way to Australia. While flying low in a sandstorm over Iraq, Bedouins shot at the aircraft, killing the engineer, Arthur Elliott. Cobham returned safely to England landing on the River Thames in front of the Houses of Parliament before a crowd of one million thronging the bridges and embankments. Immediately knighted, Cobham found himself an inter-national celebrity, much in demand both in Britain and in the United States.

Cobham duly arrived in Hereford on 12 September 1929 landing on the Lower Lugg Meadows just outside the city (the racecourse and Oldfield being regarded as either too obstructed or too small to take the aircraft) to the cheering of a large crowd. He then took city officials and 77 children, chosen by ballot, on short flights to give them their first taste of air travel. Cobham explained that his tour of 100 cities and towns was to create a greater interest in aviation, particularly in the younger generation, and in the erection of municipal aerodromes.

Deciding in 1932 that the British calendar should include a National Aviation Day, Cobham promoted the idea with a travelling airshow which became known as 'Cobham's Flying Circus'. Up to ten aircraft with skilled aerobatic pilots, wing-walkers, parachutists, novelty turns and joy-rides thrilled crowds throughout Britain, including a return visit to Hereford in May of that year and also to Llandrindod Wells in June. The spa town had in 1931 already staged the first aerial pageant in central Wales when Messrs. Linnell, Deterding and Palmer put on a show before several thousands. So the arrival was eagerly awaited of Cobham, who came with nine aircraft including the three-engined airliner 'City of Pretoria', capable of seating 16 passengers. One of the first to fly, Councillor Gwilym Davies immediately went up in another machine and 'had the thrill of looping, spinning, banking and generally doing the apparently impossible.' Trainee nurse Annie Hutt described her experience: 'I didn't tell mother but I had a ride on one of the planes and "looped the loop" over Newbridge. I was too scared to feel sick but it was worth every penny, really wonderful!' One mishap occurred when a biplane ran out of fuel and landed at Rhyd Lyn Ddu farm, crashing right into the front door, just below the Welcome sign!

Highlight for the huge crowd was wing-walking by Martin Hearne, who stood on the lower wing of a biplane, then the upper wing, before sitting on the wing with legs dangling in the air while travelling at 100mph. Finally he sat on one of the wheels below the pilot as the plane looped the loop. Cobham told members of the local Rotary Club that he was touring no fewer than 175 towns with the idea of making flying popular with the general public.

Cobham's Flying Circus returned to Hereford the following year and in 1934, and also visited Leominster and Hay-on-Wye. During the four years of its existence, the Flying Circus was watched by four million people nationwide and nearly one million passengers were taken up for short joy rides. Other aerial displays were put on in the area in the mid-1930s but never quite lived up to the shows by Cobham, who by this time was setting up other aviation enterprises.

In 1933 a new local company, Universal Aircraft Services, set up an air taxi service at the old racecourse at Llandrindod Wells. Described as 'this exhilarating and modern form of travel', the company operated

Avro and Bristol biplanes flying to destinations such as Aberystwyth, Birmingham, Bristol, Cardiff, Hereford, Shrewsbury and London. Rates were 9d each passenger in the three-seater Avro and 1s 3d in the two-seater Bristol. Joy rides were from 5s. The service lasted only a couple of years, although air displays continued at the aerodrome until at least 1937, including a Jubilee display in June 1935.

Tom Norton's interest in aviation continued. He still owned the aerodrome and for some time was considering taking up the distributorship for Wales of BAC's Super Drone, an ultra light single seat aircraft powered by a 750cc Douglas engine. To this end he was in lengthy correspondence with BAC's managing director, Robert Kronfeld, the famous Austrian gliding ace. Kronfeld even gave an exhibition of the Super Drone, described as 'flying for the million [masses]', at Llandrindod Wells. Its retail price was £275 and was claimed to have 'wonderful stability and easy control.' Eventually, however, Norton turned the offer down — a wise decision in the event as single seaters never became popular. He even toyed with the idea of selling the POU, or 'flying flea'. This was the brain-child of Mr. S.V. Appleby, who based his idea on a French design. It had a four cylinder engine with a very short fuselage and retailed at £198.

Private airfields were also being established at this time. For instance, Randolph Trafford opened one at his home, Michaelchurch Court at Michaelchurch Escley, at the foot of the Black Mountains. It was in Switzerland, where he owned a chalet, that he learned in fly on a French built Morane Saulnier monoplane, which he later flew back to England. He later bought a de Havilland Gypsy Moth. During the 1930s there could be as many as 15 visiting aircraft parked on the airfield, which had a windsock, hangar and petrol pumps. Another private landing strip in use from about 1936 belonged to Leonard Weston situated to the rear of the local garage in Much Marcle in Herefordshire. On more than one occasion Weston flew his own Tiger Moth to London to fetch urgent spare parts for car repairs at the garage.

Large crowds flocked to Hereford racecourse on 18 September 1936, not to watch horses but to enjoy the spectacle of 22 aircraft racing against each other. The first event of its kind in the area, the Three Counties Air Race attracted competitors from all over Britain. The race consisted of three laps around a 30 mile triangular course with turning points over a private airfield owned by Jack Barclay at Bredwardine and Randolph

Trafford's airfield at Michaelchurch Escley, with the finish at the west end of the racecourse. After a staggered start, about half way through the race, an eye witness said: 'A few of the biggest machines with handicaps roared by and then the crowd sat down to wait for the leader at the end of the second lap. Ten minutes went by and a speck appeared in the south-west sky. Who would it be? The Glass sisters seemed to be favourites. Then a great shout of 'It's Humble!' rent the air, and in the twinkling of an eye the great white machine had flashed down to the sock, skimmed round and set off for Bredwardine again, amid the cheers of a wildly enthusiastic crowd.'

The race was in fact won by Mr. R.F. Hall in an Avro Cadet with a time of 45 minutes 34 seconds. Second were the Glass sisters, Mabel and Sheila, in a de Havilland Moth in 48 minutes 6 seconds, while third was Mr. A.F.E. Payen in a Puss Moth in a time of 48 minutes 14 seconds. Fastest speed was achieved by Mr. M.W. Humble in a Miles Hawk Speed Six, who at one point nearly reached 200mph.

With the outbreak of the Second World War private airfields were requisitioned by the War Office or closed down altogether. In many cases concrete blocks or boulders were laid across the landing areas to prevent possible use by enemy aircraft in any invasion plans. This was the fate of Michaelchurch Escley, Llandrindod Wells and Kings Acre Road, Hereford, all of which never re-opened again.

However, other sites were opened for military use. For instance an area of flat farmland mid-way between Pembridge and Shobdon in north Herefordshire became an airfield in the summer of 1940. Originally called Pembridge Landing Ground and without hard surface runways, this airfield became operational when No.8 Anti-Aircraft Co-operation Unit moved in with Westland Lysander and Fairey Battle aircraft to support army manoeuvres. A year later, the site was upgraded with the building of proper runways and renamed Shobdon Airfield. Hedges were grubbed up and farming obstructions cleared to allow the construction of a massive triple-width tarmac runway, 300ft wide and 4,900ft long with an overrun of 1,040ft. Narrower grass runways were also built, together with a number of buildings including 12 hangars, lookout tower, workshops, administration buildings, instruction hut and cinema/entertainments building. The anti-aircraft unit moved out to be replaced in July 1942 by No.5 Glider Training School complete with Miles Master tugs and Hotspur troop carrying gliders. For the rest of the war until its closure in November 1945, Shobdon was the scene of considerable gliding activity. Some 1,345 glider pilots were trained during that time, together with 291 glider instructors and 218 tug pilots. Altogether 96,925 separate glider launches were made.

The pilots were part of the Glider Pilot regiment as they were required to fight on landing. They took part in all the major airborne operations of the war, in Sicily, in Normandy on D-Day, and at Arnhem and the Rhine Crossings. The instructors were also in the Army, but the tug pilots and maintenance crews were in the RAF and Shobdon was administered by the RAF.

The glider used for training was the Hotspur, carrying only eight men, but this never saw action. Actual operations were carried out using the Horsa glider which could take either 30 men or a combination of men and jeeps, tanks and armoured cars. There was just one Horsa at Shobdon, but this was used for familiarization only, it never flew. The tug pilots flew specially adapted Lysander and Miles Master aircraft, both powered by Bristol Mercury engines. Navigation of the gliders around the airfield was conducted by Tiger Moths and Miles Magisters. With tractors at a premium, cart-horses were enlisted to drag gliders back to the end of the runway so they could be re-attached to the tow-planes.

An accident on the night of 25 February 1944 led to Warrant Officer G. Woodson being awarded the Air Force Cross for gallantry. Woodson was the pilot of a Hotspur glider when its Master tug suffered engine failure, released the tow rope and crashed. He force-landed in the dark near the burning Master and rescued one of its occupants.

Brian Davies, DFC, who lives in Tupsley, Hereford, recalls the time when he was a tug pilot at Shobdon as a young sergeant in the RAFVR in 1943. He flew both Lysanders and Miles Masters, but preferred the former, considering it 'a tug pilot's dream as opposed to the trickier Master.'

Normally it was the glider pilot who cast off, Mr. Davies explained. On release he would turn right, the tug simultaneously turning left with the tow rope dangling behind. The tug returned to base, dropping the rope at a designated rope dropping area. A single decker bus housed the rope recovery crew who developed a technique to dodge the falling ropes. One would stand facing the approaching aircraft with his arms outstretched indicating which way he wanted it to bank so the rope dropped as near the bus as possible. As he saw the release happen, by the tug pilot's guesswork, he leapt into the safety of the bus, hoping the rope would hurtle alongside. Tug pilots sought 'bullseyes' by draping the rope along the bus roof!

Mr. Davies also recalls a series of accidents befalling a farmer who lived near the airfield's southern boundary. Several gliders had landed short in his near-ripe wheat field, and ambulances, crash tenders and recovery vehicles had badly trampled the corn. For good measure the farmer's recently repaired chimney stack was again damaged by a dangling towrope. 'He appeared on the airfield, shotgun under his arm, looking for the culprits and needed much persuasion to leave with promises of compensation.'

Another new RAF airfield was built in six months on farmland along Stoney Street near the village of Madley in west Herefordshire, and opened in 1941. Designed mainly as a school for wireless operators, it became the home for No.4 Radio School, with the arrival in November of 72 trainees, using up to 60 Percival Proctor IVs and 18 de Havilland Dominie aircraft for in-flight training. Soon afterwards No.8 Anti-Aircraft Co-operation Unit arrived from Pembridge Landing Ground at Shobdon with Lysander, Oxford and Blenheim aircraft. The three grass runways were later reinforced with tarmac over concrete slabs. One of the largest training areas in the country, the base spread over $3\frac{1}{2}$ square miles with cadets having to march several miles each day for lessons and meals, resulting in the unofficial motto 'Never have so many walked so far'! One cadet reckoned he marched 1,200 miles during his stay there.

Established to train 2,800 wireless operators (ground crew) and 1,200 wireless operations (air crew), RAF Madley increased the size of the village from 292 residents to about 5,000. After successfully completing the ground crew course, cadets went on for air crew training as a group of six in the twin engine Dominie, known as the 'flying classroom', before advancing to the single engine Proctors, which took only one or two cadets.

A properly equipped Mountain Rescue Unit was established at Madley, to reach crashed aircraft along the mountainous Welsh border country. General George S. Patton, Jnr. visited Madley airfield on 3 June 1944, and two years later Rudolph Hess, Hitler's former deputy, arrived at Madley to board a flight for Nuremburg. Hess had been held as a prisoner of war since 1941 and was returning to Germany to face trial for war crimes. By the end of 1946, the RAF had left Madley and in the

1950s various portions of the airfield were sold off to civilian buyers and large sections of the runway were eventually torn up and returned to agriculture. One part is now owned by British Telecom who operate one of the largest and busiest satellite stations in the world. On a 200-acre site, the Earth Station contains over 70 dishes carrying signals for television, telephone and internet.

A number of airfields opened in Shropshire mainly for training purposes involving thousands of servicemen and women from around the world. Aircraft ranged from Spitfire and American Thunderbolt fighters to Halifax, Whitley and Wellington bombers. Staverton in Gloucestershire served as an RAF training base, while Credenhill, near Hereford, opened as an RAF training school for technical students, including airframe and engine fitters, and torpedo experts.

Soon after the end of the war Aircraft (Hereford) Ltd. was formed with the aim of reviving civil aviation in the area. It was the brainchild of Flt. Lieut. F.H. Snell, an ex-RAF pilot, and Mr. Jim Brook, a local garage owner. To this end they approached Hereford City Council with a view to establishing an aerodrome on the Holmer Road Racecourse. By summer 1946 permission was granted and work began to clear, level and drain the central area resulting in the completion of two grass

*The first privately owned aircraft to land at Hereford for nearly seven years, reported the* Hereford Citizen and Bulletin *of 11 January 1946, was piloted by Flight Lieutenant F.H. Snell, AFC, accompanied by Mr. J.A. Brook, directors of the newly formed Aircraft (Hereford) Ltd. The machine is a civil type Auster three-seater*

*Flying display at Hereford Racecourse, June 1948. (Derek Foxton Collection)*

runways. Hangar and flying club facilities were added and a fleet of seven Austers, a Tiger Moth and two sailplanes was purchased. The Austers were civilian versions of the single engine monoplane used by the Army as a spotter plane. The official opening ceremony was on 18 September 1947 when the first charter flight also took place, which could link up with flights from international airports. Flying tuition was offered at £3 5s. an hour. Hereford Gliding Club, formed in 1936, and Hereford Aero Club, also took up residence on the racecourse.

At the end of December 1948 the company bought a further fleet of Austers, two Percival Proctors and two nine-seat de Havilland Rapides from Autocars (Worcester) Ltd., but the expansion created problems. The company became more indebted, whilst the Rapides proved too large to operate from the small grass runway. The company changed its name to Inter-City Air Service Ltd., with an increase in its nominal share capital to raise more finance, but then the restricted space problem worsened when Hereford City Council invited the Three Counties Agriculture Society to stage their 1950 exhibition on the racecourse. Relations between the aircraft company and city council deteriorated to such an extent that neither bothered to renew the airfield's Civil Aviation licence in May 1951, and by the end of 1951 Inter-City Air Services pulled out altogether.

With the closing down of the racecourse facility, other sites were looked at to provide Herefordshire with a licensed airfield. There seemed to be only two possibilities, Madley and Shobdon. However, Madley was ruled out as sections of the airfield had been sold off to private buyers and parts of the runway torn up and returned to agriculture. As for

Shobdon, the Ministry of Defence were not interested in allowing civil flying from the airfield, where the massive east/west runway had become derelict and the hangars only used to store surplus army equipment.

However in 1961 Herefordshire Aero Club was formed with former Spitfire pilot Mike Edwards as chairman. At its inaugural meeting, plans were set afoot to re-open Shobdon airfield and eventually permission was granted by the Air Ministry for the club to use the easterly end of the runway and No.4 Hangar at a rent of £1 10s. a week per aircraft. While committee members cleared the runway of weeds, Mr. Bert Bengry loaned the club, free of charge, a huge grader, and also supplied lorries and a loader to shift 200 tons of waste.

With the control tower being converted into a temporary clubhouse, the club started enrolling new members the following year, while an official licence was granted by the Ministry of Civil Aviation. Flying lessons cost £4 10s. an hour using an Auster Autocrat aircraft, and further work was done to repair the whole length of the main runway. In 1964 the airfield was sold off to new civilian owners, the northern part subsequently being purchased by Corbett Farms Ltd. with whom a lease was drawn up whereby flying could continue. In 1967 the first annual air display was held at Shobdon and a year later the first annual air race for the Strongbow Challenge Trophy sponsored by Bulmers.

Nowadays the club, owned and run by its members, operates from one of the old RAF nissen huts, which has been converted into a clubhouse with an operations room and briefing rooms, together with a café and lounge bar, both of which are open to the public. Its fleet of aircraft consists of four Cessna 152s, a two-seater trainer, and one Piper Archer, a four-seater tourer. A whole range of private aircraft also use the airfield. Membership is between 350 and 400 strong with some members coming from as far afield as Wolverhampton and South Wales. While the Air Shows stopped in the 1980s, the Air Race, now organised by the Royal Aero Club as part of a series of races throughout the country, is still held every year over a weekend in August. There is a race on both Saturday and Sunday, each of four or five laps along a circuit taking in the Milton cross-roads, Dilwyn, Upper Hill and the Leominster Car Auction site.

The Chief Flying Instructor, Dennis Davies, joined the club in 1975 as assistant to the then CFI, when there was also a manager, Jimmy James. However, five years later James left and Dennis found himself doing both jobs until the end of 2005. Dennis came to flying late in the day. Having graduated from university with a degree in civil engineering, he worked in Zambia for seven years. But one day he went up in an aircraft and enjoyed it so much he decided to learn to fly. Having gone solo in Zambia, he took his private pilot's licence in Cyprus and returning home obtained his instructor's ticket. After a stint in Liverpool, he came to Shobdon and has now logged up over 21,000 hours flying.

Training is mostly carried out on the Cessna aircraft with three part-time instructors to help Dennis. A 30 minute trial lesson on the Cessna can be had for as little as £54.50, while an hour would cost £100. To gain a Private Pilot's Licence (PPL), a minimum of 45 hours flying training is required of which 10 must be solo. The youngest age allowed to fly solo is 16 while you have to be 17 to obtain a Private Pilot's Licence, a year younger, it should be noted, than passing the test to drive a car. Dennis recalls the case of a 70-year-old man who took the course to prove to himself that he could fly solo. Once having achieved his goal, he didn't fly again.

Age does not appear to be a barrier to flying, providing the person is reasonably fit and healthy. Take, for instance, Jim Smith, the club's oldest member, who is still flying at the age of 86. During the summer months he is to be found on day flights to various places on the Continent, as pilot or navigator, in either the club's Piper Archer or in an aircraft operated by a syndicate. He joined the club 10 years ago when he went to live in Leominster, thus renewing his acquaintanceship with Shobdon from where he flew for three and a half weeks in 1942. During the war Jim flew a variety of aircraft including Lysanders, Oxfords and Wellingtons before being chosen to go abroad and put aircraft together out of crashed planes, thus fulfilling his interest in engineering. For the next four years he was based in India flying to various parts of the Far East, including Burma and Malaya, picking up bits of crashed aircraft for reassembling. 'It was quite a gruesome job,' he recalled. 'There were no body bags in those days. You couldn't get rid of the stench, especially when the bodies had been burnt.' He flew about 6,500 hours in the war, but has not kept a record since. What makes him keep on flying? 'It's one of those subjects you have to keep up with all the time. That is the driving force. You have to keep up with everything. And if you are involved with other people it keeps the grey matter going.'

Having waited for the weather to improve, it came as a bit of a shock when after phoning Herefordshire Aero Club one sunny morning in

June, I was invited to take a flight that very afternoon. I reported to the club HQ, housed in one of the old nissen huts and still redolent of Second World War flying heroics. Having completed the formalities, I waited for Dennis while he went to get some water to clean the windscreen. 'Jack of all trades,' he muttered. Then I followed him outside to our awaiting aircraft, a two-seater Cessna 152, with dual controls and the basic trainer for anyone wishing to take their PPL. From being blue skies in the morning, they were by now covered in clouds with a heat haze coming off the land. No matter.

The first problem I encountered was actually getting on board with my long legs proving the main difficulty. Once inside I realised it was a good job I wasn't obese as well as being tall, otherwise there would have been no room for the instructor! Then Dennis showed me the controls and instrument panels before going through the customary instrument checking process. 'She's a bit noisy, so we'll put on these ear-phones,' he advised. As we taxied to the main runway, he suddenly told me to get hold of the control column and then, on the runway, to push the throttle 'all the way in' as we built up speed and then left the ground.

'Keep the nose up,' he instructed, 'until we get to about a thousand feet and then level off.' As he'd alerted me, the control column was sensitive and needed gentle handling. 'Relax a bit more,' Dennis said. 'Put

*Dennis Davies, chief flying instructor of Herefordshire Aero Club, at the controls of a Cessna training aircraft at Shobdon*

the nose down a bit and then you can see where you're going.' Wowee, I'm flying, I told myself — with a little help from Dennis, of course.

We were heading towards Leominster with the Clee Hills to our left. Then underneath to our right was a vast expanse of plastic, blinking in the light, the dreaded polytunnels so favoured by strawberry growers. 'It might be a blot on the landscape, but it acts as a very good landmark to the airfield,' Dennis said rather philosophically. We turned at Leominster 'that's right, turn the control more' and were soon flying directly over the polytunnels and the caravan village, rows and rows of them for the Eastern European pickers. Then we were heading westwards with the outskirts of Hereford vaguely discernible and the Black Mountains beyond. As we approached Dilwyn, the village where I live, Dennis took over the controls and flew round it a few times to allow me to take some photographs. The church stood out and I could even see the house where I live. As usual with sleepy Dilwyn nobody appeared to be out so there was no one I could wave to!

All too soon the journey was coming to an end. 'Aim for that triangular field in between the two farmhouses,' said Dennis. Then it was a sharp right to the runway. 'I'll take over from here, but keep your hands on the column just to feel what happens.' We skimmed over the boundary fence with seemingly inches to spare and then the tarmac loomed ahead, reassuringly very large and empty. With speed reduced, we flew over it for a while before the wheels touched down and a very smooth landing. 'Piece of cake,' I boasted to Dennis, 'but I guess it was a good job you were with me.'

Over a celebratory cup of tea in the club café, I asked Dennis what flying meant to him. 'We live in a beautiful part of the world and to get a view of it which very few people get to see is a privilege. When you get released from the bonds of earth you forget about them, but it doesn't solve them. You've got to have your mind on the job, got to keep on your toes.'

As far as teaching people to fly is concerned, he delights in taking raw beginners right through the process to become qualified pilots. 'Some people just can't get the hang of it, but to others it comes very naturally,' he said. I didn't like to ask him which category I came under!

The training course to gain one's PPL covers the basic rudiments such as aircraft familiarisation, climbing, descending, turning, slow flight and circuits, culminating in one's first solo flight. This is followed by steep turns, emergency drills and instrument flying which lead on to dual and solo navigational skills. Practical tests in navigation and general handling complete the course. It is also necessary to sit some exams including aviation law and radiotelephony. The cost of a PPL course is £5,135 which includes the minimum of 45 hours flying training, although the average is about 50 hours.

After taking the PPL, one can go on to Night Rating and Instrument Meteorological Conditions rating (flying in or above cloud). And, of course, one is free to hire one of the Club's aircraft and make trips to the Continent.

Gloucestershire Airport is located near the M5 motorway, between Gloucester and Cheltenham. It began life in 1931 as Down Hatherley airfield, on a site adjacent to the present airport, when Major Blood and Arthur King, who ran the Gloucester company, Westgate Motors, needed somewhere to demonstrate de Havilland Moth aircraft for whom they had become agents. Then in 1936 the Down Hatherley operation moved to the other side of the main road, where Cheltenham and Gloucester councils had bought 160 acres of land for development as a municipal airport. Railway Services were the first commercial users when they staged through the airport on their Bristol to Birmingham run. The airfield was then taken over by the RAF and in May 1939 the Martins School of Air Navigation arrived. In September the name was changed to No.6 Air Observer Navigation School and the airport re-named Staverton. New hangars were built to accommodate the unit and its biplane Dominie trainers (the military equivalent of the de Havilland

*A demonstration of flying over the premises of the Westgate Motor House, Gloucester. The aircraft in the air is a de Havilland Moth, that on top of the showroom is an Avro. (Cotswold Aero Club)*

*The official opening of Staverton Aerodrome on 26 September 1932.*
*(Cotswold Aero Club)*

Rapide), while aircraft were serviced by Airwork Ltd, under government contract. By the end of 1940 the Dominies had been largely replaced by the radial-engined Anson. No.2 Elementary Flying Training School, later called No.6 Flying Instruction School, also moved in with its Tiger Moth biplanes. The following year the Navigation School had 53 Ansons and three Dominies and one of its flights was composed entirely of Polish airmen. A typical exercise flown by an Anson, known affectionately as 'Faithful Annie', lasted up to three hours. It was crewed by a pilot and wireless operator with three trainee navigators taking it in turns to direct the pilot. No.7 Anti-Aircraft Co-operation Unit with de Havilland Rapides and No.7 School of Technical Training also used the airfield during the war.

Staverton was also used by civilian companies such as Rotal Flight Test Department, Folland Aircraft Ltd. and the Gloster Aircraft Company Flight Test Department. Rotol, previously known as Smiths, who were manufacturers of airscrews and aircraft components, had built a new factory on the old Down Hatherley airstrip, and later made propellers for Spitfires and Hurricanes. They tested a number of prototypes including the first production Spitfire I, the Folland F3/37s, Westland Welkin, and Hurricanes, Typhoons and Tempests. Also based there was Sir Alan Cobham's Flight Refuelling company which, as the name implies, developed mid-air refuelling. It also carried out fighter towing trials with a

*Joe Lloyd learning to fly a Gypsy Moth at Staverton in 1934 with instructor Mr. J.G. Harcombe. (Cotswold Aero Club)*

Spitfire or Hurricane towed aloft behind a Wellington bomber on the end of 400 feet of rope. The idea of towing a fighter to act as an escort or increase its range was abandoned in 1944 when fuel drop tanks became available. The navigation school closed down by the end of 1944 and the last flying unit to use the airfield was No.44 Group Communications Flight, operating a variety of aircraft including Proctor and Tiger Moth. After the war, Staverton was home to the RAF Police School and other ground units before it was handed back to Gloucester and Cheltenham councils. Later regional airliners started to operate scheduled flights to the Channel Islands, Dublin and the Isle of Man, while a number of aviation companies set up business.

From 1962 until 1979, Staverton was the home of Skyframe Museum, one of the first museums to dedicate itself to the preservation of Second World War aircraft. It was founded and run by Peter Thomas, whose son, Desmond, was killed in the war. Among the aircraft on display were a Sunderland, Avro Anson, Mosquito, Tempest, Vampire and Oxford. Some of these were flyable and the Skyframe air display was one of the highlights of the airfield's calendar. After the Museum closed, the

Staverton Air Show was held every year until 1990, with vintage and modern aircraft taking part and often a display by the Red Arrows.

In 1993, Staverton was renamed Gloucestershire Airport with a new terminal built in 1999, and is now run as a company with Cheltenham and Gloucester councils as shareholders. It is a busy centre for business and recreation flying with about 90,000 movements a year from four runways. Several flying schools, both fixed wing and helicopter, use the airfield, together with Police Aviation and Bond Air Services, which both provide helicopters and aircraft for police and ambulance work. In addition, air taxi and charter flights are available and a scheduled service operates to the Channel Isles.

One of the flying schools is Cotswold Aero Club, founded in 1927 and one of the oldest in the country. It started at Brockworth, about three miles south of Staverton, which used to have an airfield, with founding members including Arthur King and Major Blood of Westgate Motor Company, and Dennis Foot. The flying instructor was Rex Walwin, of Walwin Photographers, who provided the camera used in the first flight over Everest in 1933. The club then moved to Down Hatherley, before becoming established at Staverton in 1936. One of the first users of the airfield and probably a club member was the celebrated aviator Amy Johnson, who lived nearby at Stoke Orchard. She established several long distance records with solo flights to Australia (1930), to Tokyo (1932) and to the Cape of Good Hope and back in 1936. In 1938 the club began training pilots under the new Civil Air Guard scheme, being overwhelmed with applications as soon as the scheme was publicised. The cost of the training was very low, being set at between 5s. and 10s. an hour, less than a quarter of the normal flying school rate. Its fleet comprised Gypsy and Tiger Moths, Swallows and an Avro Tutor. At that time the clubhouse was quite luxurious with silver service meals, a swimming pool and a tennis court. During the war the club kept going as a social entity in Combe Hill and re-started flying activities in the winter of 1945/46. With a company called Wyndstruments having taken over the old clubhouse (using the swimming pool for some of their experiments), Cotswold Aero moved into part of a row of three hangars and Portacabins, described as 'a shanty town.' From the late 1940s to the mid 1960s, it was run and owned by Jack Bennett, an ex-RAF pilot, who was also the flying instructor with a mixture of Austers, Tiger Moths and Magisters. From 1966 until 1983 the main aircraft were Bolkow

Juniors, to be replaced by the Robin R2100, still included in today's fleet, together with the PA-28R 200 Arrow, PA-34 Seneca and Beech 76 aircraft. From 1970 until 1995, the chief flying instructor was John Cole, who only stopped flying four years ago, two years before his 90th birthday.

The row of wartime buildings was re-developed in the late 1990s and from 1998 to 2001 the club operated from a former public house, known under the names of Red Baron, the Aviator and Airport Inn. While not quite up to the old pre-war standard, the new clubhouse contains a lounge, operations and briefing rooms, a shop and lecture room. The club is owned and run by Phil Matthews, the chief flying instructor, and (until January 2007, when she suddenly died) his wife, Chris, who was the operations manager, with a membership of between 170 and 180.

Phil, who joined the club in 1970 and took his Private Pilot's Licence, has now logged up some 15,000 hours on all kinds of light aircraft. As well as teaching people to fly, he also acts as a 'safety pilot' for private aircraft owners wanting to make business trips to various parts of Europe, and carries out air testing and ferrying for some of the airport organisations. In addition, he is a flight examiner for the issue and re-issue of flying tests.

'When you first start flying it is the magic of being up there and being able to view the world from a different angle,' he told me. 'Seen from an aircraft, a rainbow takes the shape of a full bright halo. Some people still regard it as the freedom of the skies, allowing you to do what you want.' He added: 'It's always nice to see people progressing into someone new and you get a bit of a buzz when you release them into the world of flying.'

His wife, Chris, said they regard themselves as caretakers of an aviation heritage. 'There is very much a club atmosphere here, with lots of social events', she added. 'Flying is an addiction and a love for so many people. It is also a tremendous leveller, cutting across all levels of society.' About 10 years ago they could even boast a hatch, match and dispatch trio amongst their members, or, in other words, a gynaecologist, a vicar and an embalmer. The longest serving members are Clive Roberts and Rod Ashforth, both in their 70s, who joined in 1956. John Cole, the President, is the oldest member at 90 years of age. The club also trained two young men for their PPLs who have gone on to bigger and greater things. Mark Parker, who is in the RAF, was the junior world gliding champion in 2005, while Ross Clifton, who acted as a gofer doing odd jobs to pay for his PPL, is now flying with Air Atlantique.

A 30 minute trial flight costs £65, while the lowest price for training is £128.99 on the Robin. A five per cent discount is offered for block purchase, with a PPL course of 45 hours flying training, for instance, coming to £6,395.

A recent arrival at Gloucestershire Airport is Tiger Airways, who specialise in providing flights in vintage open cockpit biplanes from the Tiger Moth era. Their main aircraft is the Stampe SV4, a Belgian plane which borrowed many features from the earlier Tiger Moth and first flew in 1933. 'We fly these rather than the Tiger Moth,' explained the Operations Manager, Chris Rollings, 'because the latter mainly have tail-skids for use on grass, while the Stampe have tail-wheels fitted and a cable operated brake.'

Among the fleet is a 58-year-old yellow-coloured G-Forc, powered by a much altered but original Renault engine with body and wings made of plywood with fabric stretched over. Then there is a G-Nife built in 1946 and covered with Irish linen, very light but very expensive at £15,000. A third Stampe, nick-named Foxy, is ex-French Navy and appeared in the film *Indiana Jones and the Last Crusade* when owned by the Hon. Patrick Lindsay, while a fourth is the latest addition. Also available is a recently acquired Slingsby Firefly, designed in the 1980s as a training plane for the British, American and Canadian air forces. Its American engine started life in a combine harvester. A good aerobatic aircraft, it is used to train people for their PPLs and carry out aerobatics at the same time. One can also get a licence in aerobatics. It has a 160hp fuel injected engine with a top speed of 180 knots and capable of continuous inverted flight. From mid-summer 2007 flights will also be available in a Stearman, used as America's basic trainer during the Second World War. People can take their PPLs on these aircraft, but the vast majority are looking for joy rides and to celebrate special occasions like birthdays and anniversaries.

One satisfied customer said: 'Much better than any roller-coaster', while an 80-year-old holder of the Distinguished Flying Cross commented: 'From two Spitfires to Stampe in one fell swoop — it was marvellous. 57 years late.' Although most flights are taken up by men, there are a number of women keen to have a go. One elderly lady enjoyed an aerobatic flight, paid for by her friends, who afterwards admitted: 'I don't even drive a car.' Then there was a girl who arrived with her boy-friend explaining how terrified she was. But the chief flying instructor, Tizi Hodson, encouraged her to take it step by step. 'Just sit in the aircraft to begin with,' said Tizi. 'Then we'll start up and taxi along the runway. By this time the girl said she wanted to go up. She then flew on her own, did a loop and a barrel roll, and landed by herself. She had a very light touch.'

Flying a Stampe costs £135 for 20 minutes and £175 for 30 minutes, while 35 minutes of aerobatics is priced at £235 and a whole hour's flight is £295.

Before setting up Tiger Airways in 2001, Chris Rollings ran a gliding operation in Colorado, USA and has been flying for 42 years. He has 12,000 hours on gliding and 3,000 hours on light aircraft. Tizi, who has flown for 28 years, worked at Staverton before joining Tiger Airways. She has carried out instruction at every level and has clocked up 13,000 hours flying time, including 5,000 hours on twin engine jets, and bush flying in South Africa and America.

I was a bit harassed when I arrived at Tiger Airways for my trip in a Stampe, having overslept and feeling wobbly in the bowel department. The challenging stare from two kestrels ensconced in a car by the entrance didn't help. 'Thinks he's a flyer, does he,' they seemed to be saying. 'Let us out and we'll show you what flying is about.' The birds belonged to Tizi Hodson, who it transpired had spent some time training and flying a hawk, kestrel and a golden eagle. In between, that is, riding horses and motorcycles and flying. 'I'll just check the aircraft is ready and then we'll be off,' she said, disappearing into the hangar. Now I must confess I have a thing about women motorists with concerns about their ability, especially when it comes to parking and reversing. What was a woman pilot going to be like? The only one I've known pretended to be a man — smoking cigars and drinking pints of bitter.

So it was with some trepidation that I joined Tizi on the apron having been clad in a white silk scarf and a Second World War leather jacket, lined with wool. With the addition of a leather cap with bright yellow ear-phones I now felt very much like a latter-day Biggles and in my mind was soon involved in aerial dog-fights against the Huns high up in the skies.

'Put your left foot on the wing — no the left one,' I heard Tizi say, bringing me down to earth as I approached the G-Nife, which had a

*A Stampe SVA of Tiger Airways at Gloucestershire Airport. (Cam - ARA)*

flying swan painted on its nose. 'Now your hand on that rung.' Inside the cockpit, I was able to stretch out my legs with the joy-stick in between. Several safety straps were clicked into position and I felt quite secure. Until that is the joy-stick suddenly crashed into my, er, lap. Tizi, from the seat behind, was going through her check routine. It was funny really sitting in the front seat as if I was in control. As if!

The propeller blades were turned and with a throaty roar the engine burst into life getting even louder as Tizi increased the revs. 'Wave your hand if you're ready' she said over the intercom. I guess I was, so I waved and the chocks were pulled away from the wheels and the aircraft taxied out past other hangars and stationary aircraft including an auto-gyro to the runway. An aircraft was coming in to land. Tizi was now on the radio getting the latest weather information. Conditions were good — it was a still day, the sun was out albeit there was some cloud cover. We waited again, a helicopter to our left, and then, engine revved up, we were speeding along the runway and up into the sky. I was glad of my warm jacket as I could feel the cold air rushing towards me with only a small windscreen for protection. Leaving the airfield behind we headed north at a speed of 60 knots, although it seemed faster. This was real flying, I thought. Looking up, I could see Tizi in a small mirror. 'I expect you want to take over the controls?' she asked. 'Yes, I suppose,' I

*Chief Flying Instructor Tizi Hodson with Biggles, alias the author. (Cam - ARA)*

responded. 'Of course you do.' Holding the joystick like a red hot poker, I gently raised and lowered it and then tried to keep it level. I could see Tewkesbury to the right and the switchback shape of the Malvern Hills. Then she showed me how to turn. 'Don't pull it up,' Tizi cried. 'It will fall out of the sky!' The plane responded beautifully, like a swan — even the thin wings, held together with struts and wire, looked dependable. Now I could make out the river Severn.

'Suppose you'd like to do some aerobatics now,' said Tizi. 'Shall I take the controls?' I almost said no, but quickly thought better of it. 'Hold on to the shoulder harness,' she advised, 'We'll do a very gentle, ladylike and graceful loop the loop.' She increased our speed to 100 knots and made sure there were no other aircraft nearby. Clutching on for dear life, the aircraft's nose suddenly went up and before I knew what was going on we had flipped right over and back again. I couldn't help letting out a blood-curdling cry, not of terror but in sheer delight.

'Did you enjoy that?' she enquired. 'Bloody fantastic,' was my response. 'Right, we'll do another one.' And then we were veering to the right, turning over and back up again in a victory roll. Wow! What an amazing sensation. Absolutely exhilarating. 'How was that?' asked Tizi. 'Brilliant.' I was so excited I didn't have time to think about my stomach or bowels but they appeared to be in good working order. Surprisingly there was no sensation of falling out of the aircraft; apparently the centrifugal force keeping me snugly inside the cockpit. I later learnt that the victory roll was used to announce or celebrate the shooting down of an enemy plane.

'Where's the airfield?' Tizi asked. 'I think its behind us,' I said. 'Right, then you can take us back home.' So I took over the controls and very gingerly manoeuvred the plane around and back to Staverton. I was still very much up in the clouds, thinking again of Biggles and dog fights. Ahead was a bank of low black clouds while to one side was a flat table of white. I remembered the engineer talking about dancing with the clouds and how they were not just flat but had interesting shapes. We flew along and over the motorway and past the doughnut-shaped building which houses the Government Communications Headquarters, surrounded with parked cars, near Cheltenham. Had they monitored our flight, I wondered. We circled the airfield before coming in to land, with Tizi taking over control. We landed — gracefully, effortlessly — on spongy grass, a helicopter coming in on the runway. I looked round and there were now three helicopters hovering just above the ground.

'We'll just stop off and get a drop of petrol,' said Tizi and we taxied over to the filling station, parked and 'turned him off.' She got out and rolled the pipe over. 'This is why female pilots wear trousers,' she said, clambering up onto the wing and filling the fuel tank which sat in between the two top wings. I also noticed bare feet in sandals. Ah well, my faith in women drivers had been more than restored. And on the way back to my car, I cocked a snook at the kestrels, still looking arrogant.

# Gliding

After the First World War, gliding started to become popular. With gliding 'meets' attracting large numbers of spectators, clubs began to spring up and in 1929 the British Gliding Association was formed to promote the sport. The first club to come into being in the central Marches was the South Shropshire and North Herefordshire Gliding Club, which in 1930 started operating in a large field by the River Lugg at the foot of Dinmore Hill. The club used a Dagling Primary glider, housed in an open shed, for basic pilot training and soon had a membership of one hundred. The Dagling and other gliders were launched down a short slope leading onto meadows by the bungee method, whereby a dozen or so able-bodied persons towed the gliders into the air with an elastic rope. One of the leading lights was Percy Pritchard, who towed the glider to Dinmore behind his MG. However, by the Spring of 1931 the club had disbanded.

*Percy Pritchard's car attached to the South Shropshire and North Herefordshire Gliding Club's glider.*
*(Tim Ward)*

One half of the original club reformed as the Shropshire Gliding Club in May 1935 with its headquarters at the Traveller's Rest inn at Affcott near Church Stretton under the guidance of Mr. A. Bowen, a pilot and army captain of the First World War. Operations continued regularly until, in September, their primary Dixon glider was smashed having stalled. Meanwhile the Hereford members from Dinmore Hill

*October 1930. Assembling the South Shropshire and North Herefordshire Club's glider at Dinmore, in preparation for the word 'Release'. (Tim Ward)*

re-grouped and by early 1936 the Hereford Gliding Club was formed. Basic training was carried out at Blakemore Hill, Haywood, a small knoll three miles south-west of Hereford. By 1937 the club had made 1,200 launches. The club decided to base itself on Hereford's Holmer Road racecourse in 1947, when an airfield was established there after the war (see pp.37-38). Unfortunately the airport closed down in 1951 and the club was left once again without a site. This position was not resolved until 1972 when a new Herefordshire Gliding Club came into being at Shobdon, started up by Tony Mavrogodato, an experienced gliding pilot from Dorset. With Keith Wilson as the chief flying instructor, the club went from strength to strength, probably reaching its peak in 1975, when there were between 75 and 100 members. They came from quite long distances away, with the club advertising in the Manchester and Birmingham newspapers. The fleet was composed of two Blaniks and a Pirat, both two-seaters, and a motor Falke, used for mid-week operations and for advanced training. There was also an Auster tow-plane.

As Phil King, one of the members, explained, other gliding clubs became established in locations on ridges which affected the club's membership, and today there are fewer than 30 members. With no ridge site, all flights are made by aerotow, gliders taking advantage of the prevailing westerly winds coming in waves from the Welsh mountains. The Radnor Forest area generates excellent wind lifts. The tow-plane takes gliders up to 2,000ft, from where they can fly around quite easily for three and a half hours.

The highest recorded flight by a glider at Shobdon is about 32,000ft (above 10,000ft oxygen has to be turned on), achieved by both Tony Maitland and Mike Costin, a visitor and one half of the Cosworth racing car business. It was Tony who encouraged Phil to take up gliding at Shobdon and the latter has now logged up 3,000 hours. Tony then became a pilot for Sun Valley Foods, flying a twin-engine aircraft out of Shobdon. One of his duties was flying batches of day old chicks to various parts of France, but only of the female sex so that the breed would remain under Sun Valley's control. After that he got a job as chief designer of a microlight manufacturing business at Shobdon, and presently operates a turbo twin for a Welsh company from Welshpool.

Although relatively small, the club is quite active all the year round and, as the chairman Dewi Edwards pointed out, having few members means that aircraft are available more frequently. The clubhouse is situated in a Portacabin, but members have use of the Aero Club facilities. Mike Dodd is the chief flying instructor and secretary.

'We do a lot of trial lessons during the summer,' said Dewi. 'A lot of people these days book on the internet and come from as far away as London and Brighton.' A trial lesson lasting 15 to 20 minutes costs £54.50, and a one-day course is £145, but these prices are being reviewed. At £135 a year, the pre-solo membership is cheaper than the standard rate, while for under 25 year-olds it is only £65. Then flights are charged at £31 for half an hour and £41 for one hour. The club now possesses a Blanik two-seater trainer glider, on which most of the training is done, an Astir two-seater trainer, a Junior single-seater, and a Rallye 180, a French four-seater used as the tow-plane. Most of the remaining gliders are syndicate owned, and parked on trailers at the far end of the runway. Not infrequently pilots from other clubs stop off at Shobdon on a day's flight and get an aerotow back to their own clubs in the Midlands and Black Mountains.

Dewi regrets not having started flying 40 years ago, having only been flying for six years. 'I got permission from the wife six months ago to try for my PPL also,' he said with a wry smile. 'I did a little bit in 1967 and came back to it just before I retired. My son bought me a gift voucher and I took it from there. I got a three months membership and spent every weekend here.'

The formation of the Midland Gliding Club in the 1930s is very much the story of one man, Charles Espin Hardwick, its founder and father. A Birmingham stockbroker, he became a keen sailor, motorist and glider pilot, despite the permanent dislocation of his back after a childhood accident. To become a pilot, he drove his 1924 Humber 90 miles at weekends to Dunstable Downs, home of the London Gliding Club, for lessons. He then met up with other glider enthusiasts from the Midlands with the intention of forming their own club. A suitable site for basic training was secured at Handsworth, Birmingham, but finding a soaring ground proved to be more difficult. Every likely looking hill in the area was scoured without success, until Hardwick came up with the idea of the Long Mynd at Church Stretton. It seemed ideal — a long hill ridge on the western edge of the Mynd facing into westerly winds, which offered splendid scope for soaring. Permission was obtained from the tenant farmer, Mr. Morris, to use a 5-acre patch, called the Sheep Walk, and heather was cleared to make a landing strip 80 yards long and

*C. Espin Hardwick, MBE, founder and president of the Midland Gliding Club. (Midland Gliding Club)*

7 yards wide. Then on 11 August 1934, Hardwick, now chairman of the British Gliding Association, and a small band of gliding experts towed his Falcon II, the earliest type of British-made soarable glider, up the steep and rough cart track to the site. The first flight was made by his friend, Fred Slingsby, a pioneer manufacturer of gliders, whose company Slingsby Sailplanes had made the Falcon. Catapulted off the ridge by bungee elastic rope into a fresh westerly wind, Slingsby soon climbed to 1200ft above the ridge. After cruising along its face to confirm its ability to provide deep, high and safe lift from end to end, he landed amidst his delighted companions back at the launching point. Hardwick flew next and cruised for 33 minutes at 600ft.

Following this success, a meeting was held in Birmingham in October to form the Midland Gliding Club with Hardwick as its first chairman. Then on Boxing Day the inaugural flying meeting was held at Handsworth with Hardwick making the club's maiden flight in a new Dagling Primary glider, costing £52 10s., just delivered by Slingsby Sailplanes.

Handsworth well suited the primary training system of the time, in which pupils were trained solo from the outset in cheap, tough primary gliders. These were catapulted by bungee first on the flat and then from the hill-top, starting with short slides or hops and ending in glides lasting a minute or more. But difficulties were being experienced at the Long Mynd. Max Wenner, who owned 5,000 acres on the Mynd, reckoned the gliders interfered with his grouse shooting and sought an injunction against this activity, which was upheld by Justice Crossman at the Chancery Court, London in March 1935. Fortunately, Wenner held no sway over land to the south of the landing strip which belonged to the Stretton Manor Estate, and the club acquired a new site of 25 acres overlooking the hamlet of Asterton. This proved just the first of several disputes over land and boundaries as the club built up the site piece by piece. Litigation proved expensive but once again Hardwick came to the rescue through his personal generosity.

In 1936 a hangar was built and a shed moved from Handsworth was turned into a workshop. Despite the bad state of the tracks leading to the site, visitors came in large numbers to witness the new sport. Training continued in a dual trainer, provided by Hardwick, which remained a leading feature of the club and helped change the attitude of the British Gliding Association to this form of instruction. The Autumn Camp in September 1937 was marked by a striking lenticular cloud formation which allowed the first wave flight to be made in the UK up to 7,100ft. (The wave effect is rather like the ripple effect of a stone bouncing along water.) This vested the Long Mynd with yet another powerful attraction.

A month later the famous pioneering woman aviator, Amy Johnson, joined the club as a country member. She promptly made her first solo flight in a Kite, and continued to fly most weekends. Johnson, the first female pilot to fly solo from Britain to Australia, was the star attraction at an advanced Easter camp held in April, 1938, when accommodation was provided for 40 pilots in caravans and tents. She achieved a height of 4,000ft in her Kite to gain the height leg of her Silver C (a second stage qualification for cross-country flying; see below). Visitors paid £20 in gate money to watch the proceedings, with another £6 towards club funds coming from autographs signed by Johnson. Just before the Second World War, which saw the suspension of all gliding activities at Long Mynd, Johnson gave an aerobatic display to the

*The aviatress Amy Johnson, on the left, while visiting the Mynd in 1938. Alongside her is the wife of the club's chairman, Mrs. Espin Hardwick. By this time Amy Johnson had become an accomplished glider pilot. (Midland Gliding Club)*

delight of a party from the Birmingham Scientific Society. Johnson, who remained on the club's books, died in an air crash in 1941. She baled out of her aircraft over the Thames Estuary, but her body was never found.

During the war the club gliders were requisitioned, trenches dug across the runway to prevent enemy aircraft from landing, and mortar and gunnery practice carried out. At the conclusion of hostilities, the club gradually resumed activities from 1946 mainly at weekends with the introduction in the early 1950s of occasional camps for week-long flying. Hardwick, now club president and holder of the MBE, planned a clubhouse but died in 1954 before it was completed.

In 1957 Jack Minsall was employed as the first full-time instructor, initially on holiday courses, and, after qualifying as a glider engineer, carried out annual overhauls of the club's gliders. He became the back-bone of the club, staying there until 1985. During his career he notched up 8,000 flights and 15,000 hours and was awarded a bronze medal by the Royal Aero Club, presented by the queen.

As Keith Mansell, club president since 1996, explained: 'The whole place has grown like topsy. Two dormitories with 12 beds on each side were built and in 1963 the accommodation block was added, which has since been upgraded internally. This allows us to accommodate people coming on one to five-day courses during the summer. In the 1970s we bought 180 acres of hill-top land for £16,000 and another 60 acres later. Today we own the whole airfield freehold, a total of 334 acres. The sheep farmer here has the grazing rights — but this means we don't have to mow the grass! It is one of the best sites and one of the best clubs in the country.' Mansell, who joined the club in 1958, was chief flying instructor from 1961 to 1968, and chairman from 1967 to 1987.

Chris Ellis, responsible for promotions, notes that the club has a membership of 184 coming from as far afield as the south coast and Glasgow. It employs one flying instructor in the winter and two in the summer when courses are held. There are also another 30 part-time voluntary instructors. The club's fleet includes a DG505 two-seater high performance glider, a K21 two-seater, and the older K13 two-seater, all for instruction, together with a Discus single seater high perform-ance and a K23 single seater medium performance glider, plus a K8 low performance or 'fun' machine, the original solo machine of some years ago. In addition there is a Pawnee tug tow-plane, an ex-crop duster; a motor glider, operated by a syndicate including the club; and a Slingsby

Sedburgh, about 50 years old and used by air cadets. There are also some 40 private gliders which live in their trailers on site.

The gliders are usually launched by the winch method, operated by Peter Salisbury, a professional, and a team of three. It has a powerful Chevrolet engine with a smaller winch to retrieve the cable. There is also the Pawnee tow-plane and the catapult or bungee launch with an elastic rope pulled by half a dozen people, executed off the edge of the ridge and for which a wind speed of 25 knots is required.

It normally takes about 50 flights to learn how to fly and land. Then before you can fly across country, you have to make two flights of 20 minutes and pass a written and flying test to gain a Bronze Certificate. When you have done that you go on a cross-country endorsement, involving navigation while solo gliding and landing in fields away from home. Next stage is the Silver C, a flight of five hours and a gain in height of 1,000 metres and then a distance flight of 50kms.

The Gold C consists of a flight of 300km and gain in height of 3,000m, while the Diamond C involves a distance of 500km and a gain in height of 5,000m. Further certificates can be obtained.

The Long Mynd is famous for three kinds of lift. It has a west-facing ridge 5 miles long and 800ft. above the valley so when a westerly wind is blowing the air is forced upwards allowing a glider to soar for hours. Secondly, there are rising currents or bubbles of warm air called thermals up which gliders can circle and climb to considerable heights. Lastly, there are waves of air created by wind crossing the Welsh mountains and valleys allowing gliders to climb to 10,000ft and higher at 400 to 600ft a minute.

In July 2005 the club were hosts to Competition Enterprise, a fun competition with imaginative tasks organised by the British Gliding Association, with nearly 30 gliders taking part from all over the country.

Chris, who has been gliding for nearly 50 years, originally flew model aircraft but then saw a gliding advert in the *Aeromodeller* and became hooked. He went on an intensive training course, but it took him another two years and a total of 36 flights before he could fly solo. 'Gliding is far more fun than flying a power aircraft [which he does as well],' he said. 'You are using your brain over gravity and I am always learning something new. And it is so quiet and beautiful up there.'

People can start to glide when they are 14 years of age and go solo when they are 16. 'Youngsters are undaunted — they learn quickly,'

Chris said. 'One was up for one and a half hours and he was flying perfectly.' Upper age limit depends on the person's health; the average age of members is over 50 years. The acceptable weight range is from about 8 to 16 stones. If a person is under 8 stone, then ballast is used, weights tucked underneath the student's seat.

Turning to me, Chris suddenly asked if I wanted to go on a flight. 'What now?' I nervously countered. 'Yes, we can fit you in before the next booked customer.' 'Great,' I gulped, not at all sure this was a good idea. Didn't I need more time to pluck up courage and steel myself for a flight into the clouds relying entirely on air? I was quickly introduced to my instructor, Walter Baumann, part-time but highly experienced, and after being signed in, we were pacing out across the grass towards our waiting glider. This was to be the high performance two-seater DG505, which indeed looked very stream-lined and sporty, all in white and made of aluminium, the slim fuselage perched between two exceedingly long tapering wings. It looked like a greyhound of the skies. Walter, a consultant engineer, first showed me the instrument panel including airspeed indicator, variometer and altimeter. 'But actually you don't need any instruments,' he said. 'All the information is outside.' Next he took me through the controls — ailerons, rudder, control stick, airbrakes and how they all worked. Then I had to be encased in a parachute in case of any structural faults or collision with another glider. The latter can apparently happen as the gliders vie for position in ascending a

*A high performance DG505 at the Long Mynd*

thermal. A more reassuring use of the parachute was that it makes an excellent cushion.

Much to my surprise, and not a little apprehension, was the fact that I was to sit in the front, right behind the nose, while Walter had to be content with the rear seat — the usual practise in training. It was a tight squeeze getting in and lying with my legs stretched out, feet touching the pedals, and the elevator stick close to my crotch. Then the seat belts were attached and I felt rather like an insect larva in a cocoon. In front of me was the instrument panel. Then the plastic canopy was fixed over us with a little side-flap for ventilation.

While this was going on the glider had been coupled to the Pawnee tug tow-plane by means of a cable. Normally the gliders are launched by a winch but today, because of manpower shortage, it was not being used. Then the tug, engine-revving, began to move, the cable taughtened and we ourselves were bouncing over a bare patch of grass creating a mini dust bowl and then, after one false alarm, we took off at 45 knots, soon followed into the air by the aircraft. So far so good, but we were still attached to something with a motor. But once we had reached about 2,000ft, Walter released the cable and we were up there on our own with just air to keep us up. Mind-blowing! Below us stretched the huge Shropshire valley, verdantly green, with a patchwork quilt of fields and occasional woods and hardly a sign of human habitation. A glorious setting to be flying over. Apparently on a clear day you can see as far as the Welsh coast to the west, Snowdon to the north, the Clee Hills to the east and the Malvern Hills and Black Mountains to the south. The cumulus clouds, which at the start of the day were low, had been steadily rising, and now formed a barrier to the blue sky above. But the sun had been out and thermals were being created. And the silence. It was almost eerie. Without the noise of an engine we could chat away quite happily without any difficulty in hearing.

There was a sort of bump underneath my seat and then a sudden drop. I could feel my stomach lurching downwards. 'Ah, we've found a thermal,' cried Walter. 'Let's circle round and find its centre.' We did this and Walter then began turning the glider in slow circles as we ascended. 'A thermal is made up of a series of bubbles as the hot air rises,' he explained. 'The trick is to find its centre and make the most of it.'

We came out of the thermal and made a wider circle over the valley. 'We'll find it again.' Walter then handed the controls over to me and put me through my paces. 'Forget about the instruments, just keep an awareness of what's going on around you,' Walter advised. 'Keep the nose towards the horizon'. The stick in between my legs was very sensitive and if I pushed it too much he would snap 'Don't let the nose drop, we're going too fast' and 'You're letting the nose go too high — we

*Riding a wave*

might stall.' I hated to think what might happen if we did stall. But it was an absolute joy just meandering about above the valley floor with an occasional glimpse of the Long Mynd airfield as a reminder of something more solid. Then he told me to take the horizon as a reference — if it was constant so was the speed. And if we went faster the wind noise would become louder. Then he talked me through rolling the glider by moving the control stick to the left or right which leads to turning the glider while banking.

Conversation turned to aerobatics, not that I was thinking of doing any at this precise moment, and Walter observed how quickly some youngsters learn these days, soaking up information like blotting paper. 'I usually ask them if they enjoy the big dipper rides and if they say yes, then we might do a few rolls and turns. They love it.' Yeh, well, I think we'll leave that until later, I thought.

'Let's find the thermal again,' said Walter. We did and I was passed the controls 'You have control,' he said. 'Now turn the stick to your right at the same time putting your foot down on the right pedal.' At his instructions, we turned and as I struggled to keep the nose level we continued turning, rising at the same time. 'Keep a look out for other gliders,' warned Walter. I did observe one, but it was far below — thankfully. With a few hiccups — 'don't let the nose down too much', etc — we slowly climbed upwards towards the clouds. It was almost mesmeric as

*Gliding near the Black Mountains*

round and round we went with my view mainly of the patchwork quilt beneath.

'You have just climbed 300ft up a thermal all on your own,' said Walter. 'Well done.' Wow, I thought, on my own. Fantastic. We came out of the thermal and soared around like a bird circling its prey and then Walter was saying it was time to land. We'd been up in the air for over 30 minutes but for me time had stopped still and I didn't really want the experience to end. We flew in a wide circle to the north-east of the airfield and then with our speed adjusted and no discernible activity down below Walter took us down. The grass suddenly rushed up towards me and we flew across it with a few bumps but very quickly the glider had come to a complete halt. We'd done it! Which was a rather selfish thought considering Walter's gliding experience. The canopy was taken off and I was helped out of the cockpit and back on to dry land.

'You should take it up,' said Walter, 'you seemed to be getting the hang of it.' With the adrenalin still flowing, it seemed a possibility. I certainly now knew how people can get hooked into this sport. 'Must have a drink,' he added. 'That's one of the things you've got to look out for — dehydration. Sometimes you don't realise how hot it gets up there.' And I needed a drink to celebrate!

The vision of two men both with a common interest in flying brought about the introduction of a gliding club in the Black Mountains. John Bally learnt to fly fixed wing aircraft in 1968, and then two years later became one of the first in the area to take up the new sport of hang-gliding. For the next eight years he practised the sport in and around the Welsh mountains before deciding to go in for gliding. But where?

To this end he met up with Derrick Eckley, a local farmer and flying enthusiast, in a pub in Talgarth, Brecon, in 1978 where they discussed the possibility of starting a gliding club. Derrick took John to see his land set 970 feet above sea level in the Black Mountains, which although affording only a short runway looked promising. They then made trial runs around the area in a J4 Auster. Flying over the spectacular Welsh mountains, both men agreed this was the ideal location and went on to form the Black Mountains Gliding Club.

'We were way ahead of our time,' said John. 'In those days no one could ever imagine flying out of a 450-yard-long runway and doing it with gliders. Because it is high up and there are no obstacles to clear we thought that our runway existed for a very long way across the valley.'

He added: 'We set a precedent, as most gliding sites were of 100 acres, and people in the gliding movement were holding their breath.'

But they went ahead and bought a Rallye, a French four-seater aircraft for use as a tug plane, and gliders, and soon fellow gliding enthusiasts were keen to join. Old barns and caravans provided the accommodation. John became the chief flying instructor and also took part in

*Looking along one of the landing strips at the Black Mountains Gliding Club site*
*(Derrick Eckley)*

*The Black Mountains Gliding Club's tug (Derrick Eckley)*

national and international competitions, flying with the British team a few times.

Since those early days the club has gone from strength to strength, and is now recognised as one of the best ridge and wave sites in the country. Seven years ago a Lottery grant of £50,000 was won to build a superb quality new hangar, to which a clubhouse was built on. This comprises a club room, kitchen, showers, offices and accommodation. In 2003, members bought the club off Derrick, including the 29-acre airfield and tug plane. There is now a full-time membership of between 65 to 70, with numerous visitors from a wide area. The club's fleet consists of two K13 two-seaters for training, a K6 and a Junior, both single-seaters, together with a Pawnee, an ex-crop spraying aircraft, as tow craft. There are also 20 to 30 privately owned gliders on the site.

'With soarable conditions on most days, we have longer average flight times — of about one and a half hours — than any other UK club,' said chairman Robbie Robertson, who has logged up 3,000 hours. 'And for the experienced pilot we can offer ridge runs and wave flying in almost any wind direction and excellent cross country options.'

He added that people learning to fly enjoyed greater airtime, too, because the local terrain provided good ridge soaring potential with training flights typically of 45 to 60 minutes. The total cost of going solo is about £1,640 on a soaring scheme, whereby after a pre-payment, a trainee can fly as many hours as they wish with no further hire charges. All flights are made by aerotow (the airfield being too small for a winch operation), but a height of only 1,000ft is needed to drop on to the local ridges.

The club height record of 31,500ft was achieved by Tony Burton in about 1990, while the long distance record is 670kms to Cambridge and back.

Derrick Eckley is still a member although he stopped flying five years ago, and John Bally, while a life member, has his own airstrip at his farm near Painscastle in Radnorshire, from where he flies a high performance powered Stemme S10-VT glider. This has a 23 metre wing span, a centrally situated engine and a propeller which unfolds under centrifugal force. It can fly at 30,000ft on power alone and travel all the way to the Pyrenees. With the wings folded, he keeps the Stemme together with a Bolkow 207, one of the best examples in the country, in a spacious hangar on his farm. It also houses another ten aircraft, including vintage and home-built, belonging to fellow flying enthusiasts.

*Founder members Derrick Eckley (left) and John Bally at the 25th anniversary of the Black Mountains Gliding Club in 2004*

From his 17th-century farmhouse overlooking a deer park, John also runs Global Gliding Expeditions which takes clients to countries like South Africa, Namibia and Argentina. For these expeditions he uses an ASH25 EB28, the highest performance production glider in the world, with a 1:60 gliding angle, which he keeps in the Alps. Among his clients are two princes from the Middle East.

Last year he led a ten-day expedition of three gliders, the first of its kind, to Saudi Arabia where a film production company was making a film, *Arabian Wings*, for TV. Support was provided by a bowser, light aircraft and helicopters. 'We flew over some amazing terrain,' said John, who had just returned from America where he became proficient to fly the world's fastest production aircraft, the Mooney Acclaim, which has a top speed of 230 knots. He is buying one for use as a support for his ASH glider.

'I love all forms of flying, but gliding takes aviation to another dimension,' admitted John. 'It presents new and different challenges where you have to draw on all the years of your previous experience. Then there is the purity of gliding and the opportunity it gives of flying in new parts of the world.'

# Parachuting

During the First World War, pilots in the Royal Flying Corps were not routinely issued with parachutes. There was a need for special chutes, especially for use at low altitudes and which could be released quickly to allow the parachutist to get out of danger. Lieutenant Alfred Bowen, nick-named Skip, who had joined the RFC after lying about his age, carried out many test jumps with one of the early chutes then in use, the Guardian Angel 150, invented by Everard Calthrop. Firstly, overalls were filled with weights equivalent to Skip's weight, harnessed to a chute and then dropped from an aircraft. If all went well, Skip would jump himself. Afterwards, he would report on the performance of the chute and if necessary modifications were carried out.

Skip made one jump which probably still stands as a low altitude record — from London's Tower Bridge on Sunday 11 November 1917. Wearing a Guardian Angel, he dived feet first from the bridge's highest span before

*Captain Alfred Edward Bowen in about 1917. (Brian Hales)*

69

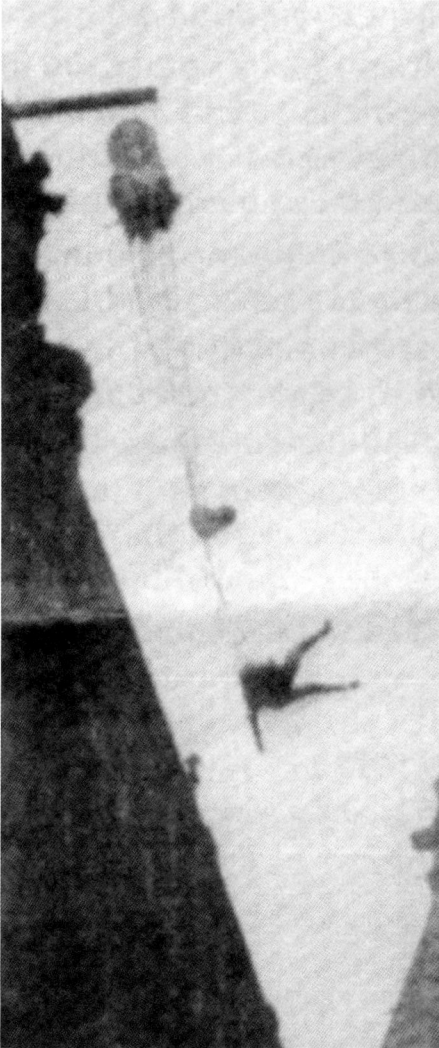

'Hon. Lieutenant A.E. Bowen, late
R.F.C., diving feet foremost. The rigging
tapes are seen fully extended; the silk body
is in the act of issuing from the container
and the air is entering its mouth.'
The caption underneath the press
photograph of Skip Bowen making the
historic leap off Tower Bridge on
Sunday 11th November 1917,
wearing a Guardian Angel parachute

'THRILLING PARACHUTE
DESCENTS FROM
THE TOWER BRIDGE.
A new parachute, intended for use from
low altitudes, the invention of
Mr. Everard Calthrop, was tested from
the highest span of the Tower Bridge.
The parachutist fell about 30 feet before
touching water.'

touching water 30ft. below. In later life Bowen moved to Eardisley, Herefordshire where one of the villagers he chatted to was Brian Hales. 'Skip told me he was made up to Captain for the Tower Bridge achievement,' said Brian, 'but that it would have been much better if he had had £200 and a bottle of Scotch.' For a while Bowen was landlord of the Boat Inn at Whitney, where he used to promote boxing tournaments and other sporting competitions, and also kept a tame fox as a pet. He died, aged 82, in November 1970.

For some years Brian longed to take up parachuting himself and eventually at the age of 28 he achieved his ambition by helping to found the Hereford Parachute Club at Shobdon in 1963. With the RAF long since departed after the war, the airfield was in a derelict condition with weeds and stones on the runways and long grass everywhere. At the time Brian worked as a fitter for Hereford County Council and his apprentice, Ken Joel, and Ken's father, Frank, were also keen on the idea. In fact Ken had already enjoyed a training jump during an Army display, while Frank, an income tax inspector, was in touch with Don Hughes, a parachute instructor and member of the SAS in Hereford. Impressed by the young men's enthusiasm, Don agreed that he and other members of the SAS parachute team, the then British champions, would give them instruction. Brian, Ken and Frank, together with Jim Green, Ron Morris, Derek Mercer, Robin Slade and Curley Ware all went to the SAS HQ at Bradbury Lines where they were soon put through their paces on landing procedures and how to roll. They were also taught how to pack their own chutes, big army ones, made of silk and 28 feet across when opened.

Then the runway at Shobdon was cleared, the clubhouse emptied of hay, and the services enlisted of local farmer, Ken Davidson, a former Royal Navy Reserve pilot, and his Piper Tripacer. Borrowed chutes were loaded onto SAS trucks and Ken's Morris van: the club was ready for action. The only specialised equipment some of them had were French parachutist boots.

'We were full of apprehension going up in the Tripacer,' recalls Brian. 'The doors and back seats had been taken out and there was hardly room for the pilot with the presence of two students and the SAS instructor. The plane only just lifted and we rose slowly to 2,000ft. Then you had to hang on to the side of the plane with the instructor leaning over you before pushing yourself out because of the slipstream. We were on a static

line and the chute opened very quickly. Then you had to check the canopy and steer with the toggles and aim for a flag on the ground. After five or six jumps we went free-fall, throwing your arms and legs out in a spreadeagled position.'

*Members of the Hereford Parachute Club before boarding the Piper Tripacer at Shobdon in 1963. (Brian Hales)*

Later the club was able to borrow a Rapide, a twin engine biplane in the blue and white colours of the sponsors, Rothmans, through the SAS, and gave displays at town shows. Jumps were made off the plane's lower wing, holding onto the struts. Accidents happened fairly frequently. Curly Ware broke a leg after a couple of jumps, Ken broke a leg at a show in Knighton and three weeks later Brian broke an ankle.

'As I was landing, the chute pulled me across the field,' Brian recalled, 'and I could see barbed wire and electric cables. I'd landed but the chute didn't, which dragged me along. Then I heard a crack. My ankle had gone. I never could land properly.' After being out of action for 12 months, he continued the sport until he had made about 15 jumps and then called it a day. Now retired, he takes pleasure in taking his boat on the river at Tewkesbury and playing the organ. Ken, who went on to make 71 jumps, left the club in 1966 when he went to Australia to continue his career as a heavy equipment fitter. Frank made his 200th jump from the Tripacer at Shobdon in the 1970s.

With the SAS becoming more covert, they pulled out of the club, leaving it to look to find a replacement instructor. One person who seemed to fit the bill was John Boxall, who had joined the club in 1968. They duly arranged for him to attend the Army Parachute School at Netheravon, where he became a qualified instructor. For the next three to four years, John was not only the chief instructor but also ran the club, which operated mainly at weekends. However, the club ran into financial difficulties and John, who worked as a mechanic at Bulmers, approached the firm's chairman, Peter Prior, with a view to the cider company sponsoring the club. The answer came back: 'No, the company won't, but I will finance you myself.' Peter not only formed the club into a limited company with four directors, but took up parachuting and even persuaded his wife and secretary to follow suit! The club stepped up its display activities at local carnivals and shows and formed a Bulmer's Strongbow skydiving team.

In 1975, John left the club to become a continental lorry driver, and was replaced as chief instructor by Mac McCarthy, who had originally helped set up the club. By then Mac had left the Army, after being an instructor for the Rhine Army Parachute Association in Germany. His two sons and daughter all took up the sport, becoming highly acclaimed skydivers.

John vividly recalls one of his students, Archie McFarland, from Bristol, who claimed to be just over 60 but later admitted to having been wounded at the Battle of the Somme and whose real age was 75. After one-to-one training, Archie went up with John's assistant 'and landed like a ton of shit.' When told he wouldn't be allowed to jump again, Archie went away disgruntled and after approaching several other clubs eventually made another jump at the Tilstock Parachute Club. In fact he made 20 jumps, the last one landing on a stack of patio slabs and dislocating his shoulder. In the meantime John had qualified as a tandem instructor, with two skydivers using a dual harness, and Archie, now aged 89, was to be the first jumper. The media heard about it and ITV sent a team. John, with Archie in tandem, jumped from 12,000ft and made a successful landing, and the whole event was broadcast on ITV News that night. The following week, John drove Archie to the Royal Aero Club in London, where Prince Andrew presented him with a special award. Shortly afterwards Archie was found dead on a Welsh mountain having set out to find the remains of a crashed German aircraft.

John also remembers the time, in 1977, when a team of Irish skydivers were jumping at Shobdon in a plane piloted by Mac, who was now running the club. One of them, Noel Farrelly, was wearing a complex parachute with twin chutes and bridle cords, and soon after deploying his main chute the cords twisted round his neck like a noose. He opened his reserve chute, but that only became entangled with the remains of the main chute.

'I watched the entire fall through binoculars,' said John, 'and just before hitting the ground there was a partial inflation of the reserve chute. Noel hit a tree, landing on a branch which bent and he fell off and into an 8ft muddy ditch. I was running across the field to him and to my amazement found he was still alive. But the bridle cord was wrapped round his neck and he was choking to death. As it happened I'd lent him a brand new jump suit which had a knife in the pocket. I was able to get the knife, cut the cord and get his tongue out. He was badly broken up, especially his legs.' Noel, an air traffic controller at Dublin Airport, was hospitalised for a year before he could walk again. But a year later, he made another jump and indeed went on to make several more.

About two years later another skydiver had an even luckier escape at Shobdon. Jonathan Vowles, son of Dick Vowles, then mayor of Hereford, made his jump only to find the main chute had malfunctioned. He opened the reserve chute, but the cords got tangled and people on the ground thought he would be strawberry jam. However, he landed on a hangar roof of corrugated iron with several Perspex skylights, through one of which he fell and became suspended above the floor by his chute. Jonathan escaped unharmed, apart from a sprained leg. A few days later, enjoying a drink in a pub, customers came over, or so the story goes, to pat his leg for luck. Later, he joined the Army and on being asked whether he would be up for parachuting, said 'not bloody likely' and joined the catering corps.

But it was a flight fatality in 1989 that led to the end of parachuting at Shobdon. A woman making her maiden flight in a light aircraft collided with a microlight and the resultant Civil Aviation investigation into the crash concluded there was too much activity going on at Shobdon. Mac, who by now owned the club, chose to close it and move to the airfield at Staverton. Although this was not cleared for parachuting, the club was based there, with the actual jumping carried out over a large field on top of Birdlip Hill, near the A417. Soon, however, Mac sold the business to Ron Loveridge, who carried on running it for a couple of years and then closed it, departing for Thailand and taking with him all the equipment. The club's regular jumpers transferred to South Cerney, near Cirencester, and jumped with the Army's Silver Stars, a local display team.

While not driving a truck, John Boxall continued to enjoy parachuting and for a few years in the late 1980s and early 1990s was chief instructor at the Parachute Centre at Tilstock Airfield, near Whitchurch in Shropshire. He even arrived by parachute at the reception of his second wedding in July 1995, accompanied by the local vicar. This was Frank Collins who had been a parachutist while with the SAS, and then on leaving the Army had become a minister. After the service at a Hereford church, at which he officiated, Frank and John boarded a Jet Ranger helicopter and skydived down onto the racecourse in Holmer Road for the reception.

Tilstock airfield, a few miles south of Whitchurch, Shropshire began life on grassland known locally as Prees Heath as RAF Whitchurch Heath on 1 August 1942, but was renamed in 1943 to avoid confusion with Whitchurch near Bristol. The main A41 Newport to Whitchurch road was closed and three runways built, two of them crossing the road, together with dispersal areas and a number of hangars. In September 1942 it became the home of No.81 OTU Bomber Command, responsible for the training of crews on Armstrong Whitworth Whitleys. A range at Fenns Moss to the west was used for bombing practice. With the OTU concentrating at RAF Sleap, two miles west of Wem, Tilstock became the base for the Airborne Forces of No.38 Group with Halifax and Stirling aircraft. Glider towing was practised with Airspeed Horsas. The activity was part of the build-up for D-Day and, later, Arnhem. Another change took place in March 1945 with the arrival of No.42 OTU to form No.1380 (Transport) conversion unit with some 50 Wellingtons, spread between Sleap and Tilstock.

In 1946 the unit disbanded and the airfield closed, with the hangars being used for the storage of equipment. The A41 was reinstated across the airfield and plans made to extract gravel from the area but, following local objections, this was rejected. A section of one of the runways was converted into a civil landing strip and then in the early 1960s the Manchester Sky Divers began using it, followed by the Manchester Free

*Open Day at Tilstock Airfield*, circa *1946. (Colin Fitzmaurice)*

Fall Club. In 1987 the Parachute Centre, in its present form, was started by Lyn George, previously chief instructor at the Cranfield Parachute club in Bedfordshire. He was later joined by Colin Fitzmaurice, who had been manager at Cranfield. In 1991 the club staged one of the biggest events in parachute history in the UK with a boogie, or fun skydiving event. Held over three days, 750 people registered to jump from two large aircraft, a Twin Otter and a Short's Skyvan, able to take 20 parachutists at a time. Two years later the club was served an enforcement notice

*Colin Fitzmaurice, owner of the Parachute Centre, Tilstock*

to close following a protest from local residents about excessive noise. However, a compromise was reached with the club agreeing to restrict operations to Friday and Saturday and Bank Holidays. Colin later left the club and went to Australia, where for six months he ran a parachute centre for a friend as acting chief instructor. 'When I came back to this country,' Colin said. 'Lyn was in the process of getting out of the club, and I ended up buying him out and taking over control.' This was in 1996. He is still there today, even living on site in a house tucked behind a row of tall trees just off the main entrance. He also works part-time as a paramedic with the ambulance service in Whitchurch.

Colin recalled how he first got into parachuting, or skydiving as it is more popularly known. 'My brother phoned me one day and said do you fancy parachuting at Ashford in Kent. It was in January 1978 and freezing cold. Despite this I enjoyed the experience and became hooked.' He sold his photographic business in London and flew to Florida, to become what he describes as a 'parachute bum', including being part of a 60 member formation flying team. He worked on a DC3 for a while as a 'grease monkey,' before returning home and getting his instructor's rating.

What is the attraction of skydiving? 'If I had to explain you wouldn't understand,' says Colin. 'It's just the rush. It affects the same sort of people who get into things like fast bikes, skiing or snow boarding. You get over the fear element. After 20 or 30 jumps it gradually goes, you know the equipment works and you get more into the technical side. Then there are your own personal goals.' Skydiving, he went on, has grown exponentially since the 1970s in the UK after Freddie Laker first introduced cheap flights to the USA, where the sport had really started. People returned with equipment and ideas, and today the divide between the two countries is a lot less.

Tandem flying, a skydive for two in a dual harness, has helped to popularise the sport, making it much easier for first-timers to jump, as the instructor does all the work. It started in 1983 in America and took off in this country a couple of years later. Before that people had to jump on their own using a static line attached to the aircraft which automatically opens the parachute as the jumper exits. Tandem skydiving is now favoured by first-timers, about 70 per cent of whom jump to raise money for a variety of different charities. The price of a tandem skydive from Tilstock is £230 on Fridays and £275 on Saturdays.

Then there are those people who want to take up skydiving seriously and perhaps join the between 50 and 60 members including a dozen women, who jump on a regular basis. They come from all over the Midlands, and from as far away as the west coast of Wales, Manchester and Liverpool. The youngest age to jump is 16, with solo free falling subject to parental permission. Maximum age is 50 (increased to 70 for tandem flights). The modern method of learning is to use the latest Ram Air or 'square' parachute. After a day's training the student makes their first jump from about 3,500ft with the chute opening automatically by static line. The cost is £200 or £180 (December to March). Yet another method is accelerated free fall whereby you jump from 12,000ft and enjoy 40 seconds of freefall guided by two instructors. This is the first in a course of 8 to 10 jumps to qualify as a skydiver.

The sport today, as Colin explained, offers a number of different disciplines, a far cry from the old days when only solo jumps for style and accuracy, involving aerobatics and landing accurately was available. For instance, there is speed skydiving with speeds of about 300mph obtained. Then there is formation skydiving, where a number of skydivers link together in freefall and competitions are held for four and eight people.

The world record for the most number of skydivers holding hands together is an incredible 400 set in February 2006 in Thailand after they had jumped from five Hercules aircraft. Even more hair-raising disciplines are freeflying, a form of aerial gymnastics including flying upside-down, and skysurfing, literally riding waves of air on surf boards thousands of feet high.

For those who want to take up the sport, parachutes, ranging from about £1,000 for a second hand one up to £4,000 for a state of the art model, can be bought. Also required is a helmet, goggles and a jump suit.

The centre owns a Cessna 206 which is used for the jumps and hires another aircraft if and when required. Facilities, housed in a row of former school rooms, include a lounge/café, a parachute packing area, training rooms and store room. The chief instructor is Pat Walters, who has been with the centre since 1994, and there are several part-time instructors.

One of the club members, Martin Lloyd, a cinema supervisor from Shrewsbury who started jumping two years ago, explained why he liked the sport. 'It's just great fun,' he said. 'It was scary to start with, but there is nothing else like it now. I should have started earlier, when I was 16.' He added: 'It has changed my life completely; I never look at the sky in the same way again. It is quite obsessive.'

My first attempt to do a parachute jump, a tandem one of course with an instructor on my back, was scheduled for 3pm on a bright but windy Friday in August. I phoned the Parachute Centre before leaving home to be told that they were running late because of the conditions but to come over anyway. Some two hours later I signed on at reception, producing a medical certificate as required for anyone over the age of 40, and was asked if I'd like to pay £90 for a 25 minute video film of the experience. While I deliberated over a large beaker of coffee, a definite comfort for slightly edgy nerves, the other person on my flight went for the video and the opportunity had gone. Surprisingly quickly I was called for a briefing with one of the part-time instructors, Tony Lightfoot, a near 3,000-jump man over a 23-year period. My fellow jumpers turned out to be a young lad, 17-year-old Tom, a last minute substitute for his father, who I understood had had second thoughts about jumping himself, and Angie, who I'd last seen behind reception, who had already done quite a few jumps.

Tony not only looked like Bill Oddie, he also possessed the same sense of humour, so the briefing was laced with lots of jokes and laughter, so much so that another instructor commented: 'This is supposed to be serious.' We all tried to concentrate a bit harder. Anyway, Bill, sorry Tony, took us through the whole procedure from the parachute we would use with one main chute and a reserve, to getting into the aircraft and landing. He assured us there was a big beautiful cushion of air as we got out of the plane. But there were two main points he stressed we should remember: the free fall position on leaving the aircraft and feet up for landing. To reinforce the message, he made us rehearse both positions. Briefing over, we returned to the lounge to wait our call. And we waited, and waited. While a couple of flights did take off and drops made, the wind worsened and flying stopped at 6pm with gusts of between 25 and 30mph making it too dangerous. I was told to report again at 10am. the following morning when hopefully conditions would be better, but Tom and his parents were unable to make it and would have to come back another time.

So back I went to Tilstock airfield the following morning where again the centre was a hive of industry. The windsock, I noticed, was blowing merrily. One of the pilots, I was informed, was late. New to the airfield, he had got lost. And there was a full list of people already booked in before my flight could be fitted in.

As I waited patiently, a video on a loop played a montage of parachute jumps, while people munched sausage sarnies and drank coffee, and children buzzed around. Outside, in the spectators' area, families craned their necks to watch their loved ones slowly descending under colourful chutes, and snapped pictures. The centre owner's dog happily paraded around. A bunch of strapping military types sauntered into the centre — an army display team en route to give a display at the Shrewsbury Flower Show.

Lunchtime came so I had a sandwich and another cuppa, more out of boredom than hunger, and then I heard my name over the tannoy. This is it, I thought. Here we go. It was time to get kitted out with flying gear and meet the other guys, two instructors, one other first-timer like myself, and the photographer. My instructor was to be Chris Gilmore, who had jumped 4,000 times during 29 years jumping since the age of 18. He was one serious fellow, not at all like Bill Oddie. My partner in adventure was Ali Young, both by name and in looks who was on a sponsored trip. Her instructor and guardian angel was Martin Wilshaw, a robust ex-army jumper with 6,000 jumps and 30 years experience. Joining us to make the video was cameraman Simon Wilkinson, another seasoned campaigner. Ali and I climbed into jump-suits and harness and then donned soft helmets with goggles and gloves. Now I was feeling the part. The moment had at last arrived. We moved to the pen outside for a final check on the gear and then to the waiting aircraft, the Cessna 206 painted a bright purple, engine already starting. All five of us climbed aboard and sat on the floor with the side window remaining open, before taxiing to the runway. With a final engine roar we sped along the tarmac and up into the air for the 20 minute flight to 10,000ft. Well, this was really it. I couldn't back out now. After closing the side window at 1,000 feet, Simon gave us an encouraging smile and the thumbs up sign. I looked at Ali who seemed as apprehensive as I was. Whitchurch came into view as we climbed higher and soon we were at 3,000ft. — still another 7,000ft. to go. I looked around the fuselage. Insulating tape along the sides didn't breed confidence but Simon assured me it was to cover any rough edges which might snag our suits. Two stickers weren't very reassuring either — 'No Fear' and 'Don't Push Meee!!' Someone had a sense of humour. As we climbed through the clouds, it became noticeably colder. I dismissed thoughts of danger and madness, but then found myself thinking about my stomach and bowels. Why did I have baked beans on toast last night? Perhaps I shouldn't have eaten a bacon and fried egg sandwich for lunch. Too late now. My instructor ran through the instructions again, but I could hardly hear him — I thought I knew what to do, however. And I had to sit on his legs with my harness attached to his. I was now entirely in his hands so to speak. Soon, all around us, as far as the eye could see, was a mass of cloud looking like some massive ice-floe, substantial and slightly forbidding. My breathing started to get faster. Keep your cool Hobbs. You can do it. Then we were above the clouds.

All too soon, the okay call came and the window was opened again, and I was told I would be the first out. Oh, God, not me! I moved towards the opening. Not yet, said Chris. And don't forget feet under the plane, hands on harness and head up. Someone shouted go and one minute I was inside the aircraft, the next I was out and hurtling through space. Ayee! It was simply unbelievable. I shouted in joy or terror — a great rush of adrenalin pumping through my body. What might have been

*Leaving the aircraft on my
skydiving experience*

someone's nightmare turned out to be my delight. My exhilaration. As we hurtled down the air noise was loud. I managed to check my free-fall position, legs crossed, head up and with a tap on my shoulder my hands in the hands-up position. Then all of a sudden our descent, at something like 120mph, was suddenly arrested when Chris pulled the rip-cord and the main chute opened. It seemed as if we were going upwards and I was reminded for the first time of being attached to Chris, my harness digging in especially under the crotch. Oops. We had dived 5,000 feet in about 30 seconds. Wow!

The howling noise stopped and all was peace and quiet as we gently descended under the billowing chute. We could even chat. I looked straight down and all I could see were my legs and then miles and miles down to earth. What a sensation. Almost giddy-making. The last bit took a bit longer, about seven minutes. It was still windy and Chris tacked the chute as we came lower. We were over the main road with cars speeding by and a few houses getting larger, then over the airfield and I could make out the centre as we came into land. One last tack and we came into the wind with the volunteer 'catchers' ready to meet us. One last instruction from Chris — lift your feet up and I did so with hands behind my knees. We almost landed on top of Simon, still valiantly photographing, but he escaped just in time as we made, what to me, was a perfect landing, just a slight bump and I was on my back. The chute was grabbed by the catchers so that we wouldn't be dragged along or even bounce back up again, and the harnesses unclipped. It was all over, a memorable experience, one I'll never forget. I grabbed Chris by the hand to thank him and then marched back to the centre with Ali, both chuckling and giggling like school-kids.

'Really fab,' said Ali. 'What an amazing rush to the head. When I saw you go I thought "it's a piece of cake," but then when it was my turn I thought what am I doing! What am I just about to do!' She even admitted she wouldn't mind doing another jump.

Well done Ali and hopefully she will have raised the £2,000 she needs to sponsor her on her Christian charity YWAM, or Youth With a Mission, project. She had left her job as a sister at the Royal Manchester hospital's children's cancer unit to spend three months in Brazil from October to January to help the street kids and HIV Aid orphans in Belo Horizonte. She hopes this may lead to a longer term nursing engagement later on.

A final word from Chris, busy repacking the chute, who told me he had encountered all types of prospective jumpers during the few years he had been acting as a full-time instructor, including a lady who had been in an air crash and two motor-cyclists who had also been involved in accidents. A somewhat bizarre case was that of a woman who bought her husband a jump because he wouldn't climb a ladder to redecorate the outside of their house. A father bought his son a jump for his 21st birthday but the son refused to jump.

Why does he like his job? 'Its much better than working in an office or factory, and the family can come along and enjoy a day out. The only thing I don't like is the weather in the winter.'

Still on a high, I drove home feeling quietly elated.

# Helicopters

The man mainly responsible for introducing the helicopter to the world was the Russian aviation pioneer Igor Sikorsky. In 1909 he built two rotary-wing aircraft, both of which failed due to lack of power. Sikorsky turned his attention to fixed wing aircraft and came up with the first multi-engine aircraft, the four-engined 'The Grand,' which had an exterior catwalk atop the fuselage where passengers could 'take the air.' Fleeing the Russian Revolution, he made his way to the United States where he started his own company, producing the famous Flying Clippers which set records for the fastest trans-Atlantic passage. He then turned his attention once again to the helicopter and in September 1939 flew his VS-300 a few feet above the ground. This was the world's first practical helicopter. Its success led in 1943 to the R-4, the first production helicopter, followed by bigger and better machines.

Used in a limited way at the end of the Second World War, by the time of the Korean and Vietnamese wars helicopters were widely used by the USA, since when they have been developed for other purposes such as rescue services, police observation and passenger services.

The appearance of civil helicopters in the central Marches did not take place until a relatively late period. Probably the first were those flown by Freemans Aviation Ltd, based near Stourport in Worcestershire, which carried out inspections of oil pipe lines in the 1970s. It originated from a plant hire business started in the 1960s by Barry Freeman and his younger brother Howard. To quickly reach customers, for instance Phizers in Kent, they bought an ex-Army Auster, which they both learnt to fly, but then found it still took time to get from the airfield to their work place. So they invested in a Brantly B2B helicopter, which they found invaluable after winning the contract to carry out the pipe line inspections. These run from Haverfordwest in Dyfed to terminals in the Manchester and Nottingham areas.

'In those days people were worried to death about helicopters,' said Barry. 'Even before we'd brought the helicopter home, a lady councillor stood in our yard and complained "these machines make a form of suction and will suck all our sheets up off the washing line." Others were concerned about the noise.'

Despite these objections, the Brantly was soon flying over Worcestershire, Shropshire and Herefordshire as it covered all three legs of the pipe line. 'We had to check every two weeks to make sure nobody was digging on or over the line,' Barry explained. 'One time we discovered a farmer actually trying to dig the pipe out with a JCB. When we intervened, the farmer was furious but soon changed his tune when I told him what might have happened if he'd pierced the pipe.'

The Freemans were soon buying more helicopters — four ex-military Bell 47s, known in the Army as Sioux, and another Brantly, a five-seater 305. To start with, the brothers landed in their plant yard but as the fleet grew they built a helipad, with hangar and fuel, in a nearby farmer's field.

The Freemans were also pioneers or forerunners of police helicopters and air ambulances. They used a Bell 47 for a police contract to carry a policeman, especially at weekends, to control traffic when the M5 motorway in Worcestershire was being widened from two to three lanes. Two helicopters were also used for crop spraying, but this was soon abandoned when it was discovered that the chemicals involved were eating away the machines' metal. Others were hired out, particularly for ordnance survey work, while yet another use was to fly ITV and BBC film crews over the scenes of traffic accidents.

After about six years both pipe-line and police contracts came to an end in the late 1970s, and by 1986 aviation activity ceased and the helicopters sold off. However, one Bell was kept which has been used by Barry's son, Neil, who learnt to fly with Tiger Helicopters, and who is continuing the family tradition.

It was not until 1992 that the first helicopter operation, which offered flying lessons and pleasure trips, was established in the area. This was Tiger Helicopters established at Shobdon Airfield, Herefordshire by Alan Ramsden. It started in a small way but has blossomed into a flourishing business.

*An Agusta of Tiger Helicopters (Tiger Helicopters)*

Originally Alan intended to be a fixed wing instructor, having started to fly in 1977 with the Herefordshire Aero Club at Shobdon, and taken his private pilot's licence two years later under the guidance of the club's chief flying instructor, Dennis Davies. But in 1983 he had a 5-minute pleasure trip in a Jet Ranger helicopter in Kent and was hooked. He sold his house, car and share in the family business, and made the decision to go to America for four years. In Los Angeles, he learnt to fly a helicopter and then became a helicopter instructor. The next three years was spent instructing and being a commercial pilot, including some work for the Los Angeles police department and charter flights. On returning home, Alan spent two years at a helicopter school in Kent converting all his American licences to British ones and becoming an examiner as well. He was now ready to set up on his own. He went back to Shobdon and approached Dennis Davies about setting up a helicopter operation. This was agreed by the club, now running the airfield, and the airfield owners, Corbett Farms, and Alan was in business. On starting Tiger Helicopters in April 1992, he rented a Porta-

*Tiger Helicopters at Shobdon (Tiger Helicopters)*

*From top to bottom a Robinson R22, Agusta and a single Squirrel AS350 of Tiger Helicopters. (Tiger Helicopters)*

cabin behind the control tower and leased a helicopter in which to begin training. However, he found that people did not want to train if there was no permanent helicopter to fly in.

'I realised I had to get a helicopter myself,' said Alan. 'When I was in Los Angeles I had flown a helicopter made by Frank Robinson and only available since 1979.' He decided to buy a Robinson R22 — which in time became the world's best-selling chopper — and his company was approved as a Robinson service centre. By now the business was also using the old parachute club building, half nissen hut, half hangar, and derelict, which he renovated with the cost being knocked off the rent. Then he decided to build a new hangar, to his own design, which was constructed in 2003 at a cost of £500,000 with 14,000sq ft of space accommodating up to 50 helicopters. Today he owns a fleet of eight helicopters: four Robinson R22s, one Robinson R44 four-seater, one Bell Jet Ranger five-seater, one Twin Squirrel five-seater, and one Italian designed Agusta 109 eight-seater. Twenty staff are employed including the Head of Training, Don MacDonald, who has logged up 17,000 hours, and six instructors, two of whom are examiners together with Alan.

The broad spectrum of operations covers flight training, charter flights, engineering and sales.

About 20 people a year are trained for private pilot, commercial and instructor certificates, together with instrument rating. Also, six police officers from Kuwait, with no previous flying experience, are currently being trained to become pilots using a helicopter equipped with video camera, infra-red and thermal imager providing an authentic police background. The company has won a second contract with the Kuwaiti government to train a further ten officers.

Charter flights, mainly using the Agusta 109, take passengers all over the country including members of the Greek Royal family, who are flown from their homes in London to holiday parks and race-courses. Then there are business trips and special occasions including weddings when the bride and father are flown to the church, or a group of people taken to a hotel for a prom night. Gift vouchers are available for that special occasion like Christmas or birthday with half-hour flights being offered.

The engineering side was started up four years ago with the new hangar providing one of the latest state of the art facilities in the country. The building is fully insulated with roof lights and lighting, ceiling fans and a main gas heater for comfortable working conditions. Mobile shelving make working bays bigger or smaller. Workshops include specialist tooling, such as a calibrator for air speed, altitude and vertical speed indicators, for the different helicopters. There is even a 'clean' workshop where the manuals are kept and a library. Three precision engineers and an apprentice are kept busy.

Getting the sales and marketing department set up has been the latest accomplishment which will help yet further promote the company. Any kind of helicopter can be bought — a Robinson R22, for instance, costs anything between £35,000 second hand and £120,000 new.

Part of the new building houses the main offices, entered through a spacious reception area, including a crew room with kitchen and viewing balcony, a pre-flight planning room for charter flights, sales and

*Instructor Gareth Abbott by a Robinson R22 at Tiger Helicopters*

marketing offices, accounts, four one-to-one briefing rooms, training and lecture rooms, and showers.

The flight training school is still housed in the original nissen hut, which has been refurbished including a suspended ceiling. A feature of the main reception, off which are briefing rooms and offices, is a hall of fame, or rogue's gallery, with pictures of all the trainees, usually celebrating with a bottle of champagne, many of whom have gone on to become successful helicopter pilots around the world.

The latest addition is a simulator, one of only a few in the UK, a custom built fuselage shell of an Agusta 109 used for advanced training on instrument rating and multi-crew co-operation. The student sits in the front with the instructor stationed behind, while five visuals project images of the flight path, which could be anywhere in the world, and the instrument panels display the simulated readings.

Tuition is carried out in the Robinson R22 with a trial lesson costing £99 and a one-day introduction to flight training £630, including three hours at the controls. Taking a Private Pilot's Licence, requiring a minimum of 45 hours flying including 10 hours solo and seven written tests, costs a total of £10,350.

Accommodation for trainees is provided in fully furnished mobile homes, or rooms can be booked at the Bateman Arms, Shobdon, owned by Alan. It once served as the local pub for servicemen stationed at Shobdon airfield during the war. Just before the D-Day landings, a number of pilots signed their names on the ceiling of one of the landings, but unfortunately the signatures are no longer visible. But one reminder of those days is a bracket clock in the main bar which used to reside in the officers mess.

Looking around his rapidly expanding business, Alan admits 'I just love helicopters. Their ability to land in someone's back garden is great. They give you fantastic freedom. Not like in some countries. In Germany, for instance, you can only land at an airport and in France there are tough regulations.'

It was a glorious winter's day, cold but sunny, when I returned to Shobdon to make a closer acquaintance with a helicopter, in particular the Robinson R22. At the training centre, I met up with my instructor, Gareth Abbott, just returning from a flight with a young student, who beamed a big smile and exclaimed: 'It was great fun.' When he heard I was the next one to go up, he added: 'You'll really enjoy it.'

Encouraged by such a positive attitude, I followed Gareth out to the chopper, sitting patiently on the hard-standing. It was a two-seater, with a height ceiling of 8,000ft and a cruising speed of 75 knots and a top speed of 105 knots. At my request, Gareth explained in some detail how a helicopter works. Its dominant feature is of course the rotor system, with two or three blades, on top of the fuselage: this provides both lift and forward motion and takes the place of the wings and propeller in an aircraft. Its chief advantage over the aircraft is its ability to rise vertically off the ground and to hover in mid-air. It can also descend vertically, but more usually lands at a gliding angle.

The engine is mounted behind the cockpit and is connected by clutch, gearing and shafting to the rotor. To counteract the twisting action of the rotor which rotates the fuselage in the opposite direction, there is a tail section with a small propeller. 'Or', as Gareth explained 'it acts like the feathers on a dart.'

Of more immediate concern was the workings of the three primary controls — the collective lever, the cyclic stick, and the two foot pedals. The first one, situated like a car's hand-brake in between the two seats, changes the pitch of the rotor blades thus enabling the helicopter to climb or descend. The cyclic or share stick, positioned horizontally and giving control either to the pilot or student, tilts the rotor disc in the desired direction and controls speed; while the foot pedals, connected to the tail rotor blades, combine with the cyclic to turn left or right.

As we climbed on board, Gareth pointed out that helicopters were far more difficult to fly than planes because they were totally unstable. Someone, he added, had described it 'like sitting on spaceballs, rubbing your belly and touching your head at the same time.' That ruled me out, anyhow.

Before putting on our ear-phones, Gareth checked out the text messages on his mobile. 'Good, got one from Duncan,' he confided. 'He was taking his cross-country solo as part of his PPL and has landed safely in Swansea. He's only a young lad and wants to go all the way and become a commercial pilot. Amazing how quickly these youngsters learn.' That rules me out again!

After showing me the instruments on the panel and what they did, my instructor started the engine and then told me to lift the collective lever. As I cautiously did so, the machine rose up. Then pushing on the cyclic stick we moved forwards — we were airborne. We headed out across the runway to the grass, where Gareth brought us down. Then we took off again, this time backwards! Can you imagine? Flying backwards. It was a strange sensation. Then we swept around in a circle and suddenly lifted rapidly off the ground at the same time going forward. Another great feeling. As we levelled off, Gareth explained that while in a fixed wing aircraft you kept the nose pointing at the horizon, in a helicopter it was the gyrocompass. Again, unlike in a plane where you could take your hands off the controls to check out a map for instance, in a helicopter you had to keep your hands on the controls all the time.

We headed towards Clee Hill over green fields and then a forest, following a ridge of trees up and over the other side. Coming to more fields with a track, Gareth took us down and almost landed. 'You couldn't do that in a plane. In this, we can land practically anywhere, providing you've got the owner's permission.' I rather got the impression that Gareth preferred flying choppers. This Robinson was certainly a very versatile machine and a bundle of fun.

We continued on, admiring the beautiful countryside with superb all round vision through the cockpit. Then we came to Ludlow and we stopped dead, just hanging there motionless allowing us to sit there in the air and admire Ludlow Castle, which is indeed a magnificent sight. 'You can't do that either in a plane,' he said. You certainly could not.

He then told me to put my foot down on the left pedal at the same time as pushing the cyclic stick to the left. We swung gracefully over in that direction and then flew over more fields until I could make out the majestic Downton Castle, with its Gothic style towers and battlements and landscaped gardens. Built by Richard Payne Knight in the 18th century, it is still privately owned, a very salubrious looking residence which apparently does business with Tiger Helicopters taking guests there during the shooting season.

As we continued on along the River Teme winding through a wooded gorge Gareth said: 'You like it, don't you, I can tell.' I could not agree more. We flew over more forest and then heading back towards Shobdon there was the terrific sight of mist in the valleys with behind the purple of the Malvern Hills and the Brecons with in between the Sugar Loaf near Abergavenny standing in solitary splendour.

We came in at a fairly steep angle to land on the grass, but then Gareth performed a few more tricks reversing and whirling round and as I broke into a big chuckle, he said: 'You're really enjoying this, aren't you. I can tell.' I had to admit that this was really fun flying and the Robinson was a great little machine. But Gareth still had one trick to play as we went back to the hangar area. Over our appointed landing spot, he kept the helicopter in hover, the machine hardly moving out of line. 'How long can you keep that up?' I asked. 'For a long time, or as long as the fuel lasts,' was the reply. He thought about letting me have a go, then thought better of it. 'It wouldn't be fair on you,' he said. 'It's all a question of co-ordination between hands, feet and brain. Some people take hours and hours before they get it right.' One of the skills, I thought, that makes flying a helicopter a lot more difficult than it looks.

I wore the happy beam on my face back to the training centre, where someone commented: 'Yes, I think he enjoyed the flight.'

Over a cup of coffee, Gareth told me that he was an instructor only at the weekends — during the week he runs his commercial photography business in Aberdare. He learnt to fly fixed wing aircraft in the United States while working as a photographer on a cruise ship and became an instructor. But then he read a book, *Chickenhawk* by Robert Mason, about the author's experience of flying helicopters in the Vietnam war. 'I thought I would like to try flying a helicopter. I tried it. The injection was given. And the rest is history, so to speak.'

Returning to this country, he started his photographic studio in Aberdare at the same time joining a syndicate and spent thousands of pounds on flying. He has logged up a total of 1,200 hours on helicopters and 400 hours on fixed wing aircraft.

Why does he like flying so much? 'Just to be in the air, I suppose,' said Gareth. 'The very essence of being airborne is divine. It is an instant gratification. And, as an instructor, to see people like Duncan going on to a standard that he can fly on his own lifts your spirits.'

Overhearing our conversation, another pilot gave us his opinion. 'My wife says I am much nicer to live with after I've been flying.'

On the way home I thought how wonderful it would be to have a helicopter parked in my back yard available at a moment's notice to pop off somewhere maybe for a day at the races, or lunch at some country hotel. We can but dream, I suppose!

# Microlights and Hang Gliding

Francis Rogallo, an American aeronautics project engineer, had a dream. He wanted to create an aircraft which would be simple and cheap enough for anyone to fly. Working in his spare time and helped by his wife Gertrude, he eventually came up with a self-inflating flexible kite called a flexible wing, which he patented in 1948. Basically it was a delta shaped wing, consisting of two sails joined along a central spar. There was no fuselage and no moving surfaces. For the next six years, the Rogallos tried unsuccessfully to interest government and industry in the wing.

Then in 1957 the Soviet Union sent up the first satellite, Sputnik 1, and a space race developed between that country and the United States. In the early 1960s America's NASA looked at ways of returning the first space capsules safely to earth after re-entry from the upper atmosphere. Rogallo saw his opportunity and soon his flexible wing was being rigorously tested for its aerodynamic qualities. However, in 1967 NASA decided to use round parachutes instead and dropped the idea of using Rogallo's wing.

Photos of the wing, however, appeared in newspapers and magazines around the world, one of which was seen by an Australian electrician, John Dickenson, who had been asked to design a kite for a water show to carry a water skier aloft while being pulled by a boat. Without any detailed plans, Dickenson worked from the photo to build the first modern hang glider. It had a wooden leading edge, aluminium crossbar, and was covered in plastic sheeting sail.

Soon other hang gliders were being built, often from just bamboo sticks and polythene sheets lashed together with bits of rope, and a new sport took off along the sand dunes of the Australian east coast in the late

1960s. For the first time free flight was available to anyone who wanted it. In Rogallo's home country, flying enthusiasts also saw the potential of the flexible wing and developed the design into hang gliders which soon manifested themselves on the west coast of California.

Hang gliding soon spread to the UK, where in this area some of the early pioneers, mainly young daredevils, were 'having a go' by jumping off hill-tops such as Hay Bluff, the Malvern Hills, the Long Mynd, and in south Wales.

In the early days hang gliding was regarded as a dangerous sport because the gliders were relatively easy to fly without instruction. Pilots are suspended from a hang strap, hence the name, connected to the glider's frame and by shifting their weight they can control the machine. Hang gliders are usually launched from a hill-top or slope but can be towed by trucks, stationary winches and ultralight aircraft. They normally use ridge and thermal lift to gain altitude.

It was not long before ways of attaching power units were tried and after much experimentation the forerunners of the modern flexwing microlight took to the skies in the early 1970s. Often called a weight-shift or trike and looking like aerial motorbikes, the flexwings are simple, robust and can be folded up and stored at home.

Then there are the fixed wings, or three axis microlights, which are more or less conventional looking light aircraft with rigid wings and a tail with movable surfaces to control flight. And of course with an enclosed cockpit.

In the meantime, standards were being laid down by the Civil Aviation Authority (CAA), who in 1978 began introducing certificates. Soon afterwards the British Microlight Aircraft Association (BMAA), approved by the CAA, was set up with powers to control training and airworthiness. Today it looks after the interests of microlight owners.

One of the first microlight schools to open in the southern Marches was at Shobdon airfield in Herefordshire. It was set up in the 1970s by John Hollins and known as Microflight, with the emphasis on flexwings. During his time there, John helped popularise the sport by training numerous people to become microlight pilots and running a successful club which offered after training facilities.

In 1984 seasoned hang glider and microlight pilot Gordon Faulkner joined up with John Hollins, who persuaded him to become an instructor. It took him six months to qualify when he joined Microflight and he then stayed at Shobdon until 1990. As a young man, Gordon had learnt to fly fixed wing aircraft before going to Australia in 1969 where, in the early 1970s, he became interested in hang gliders — 'extremely crude affairs with baggy wings' — which he rode on the sand dunes.

Returning to the UK he went hang gliding in the southern Welsh mountains, Long Mynd and Malvern Hills. In 1979 he joined the Tredegar (Gwent) based company, Hi-Way, formed by Steve Hunt and John Ivers, where the very first microlights in the UK were being made. Also working there was Frank Tarjiani, who made the first trike from a picture he saw in the French magazine *Vol Libre* or Fly Free. Gordon flew it first as a hang glider, when it became clear it was going to work with an engine. At the same time Steve was working on the first Pathfinder engine and so the hang glider and engine came together as a microlight. 'It was really like the early pioneering days,' recalled Gordon, 'to re-invent flying or finding alternative ways of flying.' Then he and Frank flew the first microlight from Tredegar to Wellesbourne, near Stratford-Upon-Avon. He continued working for Hi-Way full-time until 1982 when he worked on a contract basis and also with Mainair Sports in Rochdale. Then in 1983 Hi-Way went bankrupt and Gordon chilled out for a year until joining Microflight at Shobdon.

In 1989 Gordon was involved in a fatal accident at Shobdon. He had just taken off in a microlight with John Harris as passenger and climbing away when a light aircraft, piloted by Pamela Wilson, on her first solo flight, also took off and crashed into the back of the microlight.

'I remember being locked together with this aircraft and then one of my wings fell off and went spiralling down like a sycamore seed,' said Gordon. 'Our rate of descent was not that alarming but on impact I was knocked out. John shouted to me to get out as the fuel might catch light and we crawled away on our hands and knees from the mangled micro-light. Then we saw this Cessna buried in the ground.' Mrs. Wilson was dead. Gordon, suffering from concussion and a couple of broken fingers, and John, who had a broken ankle, were taken to hospital. Gordon was released the following day and went back to work. He stayed until 1990 when John was involved in an accident. Coming into land on a field near Ross his microlight hit a power line and crashed. Although unscathed himself, his student passenger sustained serious injuries to both legs. This led to John leaving the business. Gordon opened a microlight school with a partner at Fradley, near Lichfield and then later his own school at

Otherton, where today he trains people on both flexwing and fixed wing machines. He is presently making his own microlight from a kit which he will fly in his retirement.

'Microlighting still has an appeal,' he said. 'It is more immediate, a rawer way of flying than in a light aircraft.'

The Shobdon business was carried on under the name of Sabre Air Sports for a year or so by Peter Truscott before he sold up and went to the United States to learn to fly helicopters. The company was taken over by Brian Marsh, who had obtained his instructor's certificate in microlights at Shobdon and then worked as a part-time instructor for Peter while working on North Sea oil rigs.

He recalls the early days of hang gliding in the 1970s and flying from the White Cliffs of Dover while working for Townsend Thoresen ferries, and from the Long Mynd in Shropshire. 'It was the ultimate flying experience,' he said. 'It was real flight.' He then bought a trike unit and added an engine and flew it with his seven year-old son on his lap.

After 18 months, Brian sold Sabre Air Sports in 1994 to Steve Jones, who has been running the business with his wife, Gerry, ever since. He first started to fly gliders at Shobdon ten years previously but then saw one of the first microlights and after a trial flight fell in love with it. A few years later he obtained his instructor's certificate.

*Steve Jones, owner of Sabre Air Sports, Shobdon with his Eurostar fixed wing microlight*

'It was amazing how much microlighting had developed since the 1970s,' said Steve. 'First the flexwing became very safe and strong and allowed people from all walks of life to get airborne. And now the three axis machines are out- performing most light aircraft.'

Shortly after taking over the business, Steve decided to concentrate on fixed wing machines and trains people on one of the latest examples, the Eurostar. 'One of their great attributes is that they can take off and land in a very short distance with the maximum power to weight ratio — about 150 to 200 yards. And with their rugged endurance they can land on relatively unprepared surfaces. A lot of people use them from private landings. In fact there are thousands of farm strips in this country on which you can land providing you get permission.'

Steve went on to explain that microlights operate on a permit to fly certificate issued through the BMAA, which is renewed annually. Microlights can be de-rigged, the wings removed and stored in barns or sheds. As part of gaining the certificate, the pilot is approved to de-rig and also to carry out the maintenance on the aircraft and service the engine. The BMAA has its own engineering department and handles all training and instruction.

'We are now using very lightweight, high performance engines specially designed which give very good economy,' he went on. 'For instance, I can fly at 100mph on 9 litres of unleaded fuel, rather than Avgas, an hour, whereas a fixed wing aircraft would burn 21 litres an hour.'

He felt that microlights give people much greater freedom. There is a wide range of prices to choose from: £4,000 for a second hand flexwing, up to £45,000 for a brand new fixed wing. And the costs were similar to that of running a second family car. 'They are very safe, provide a lot of freedom and require a great deal of involvement. Part of ownership is knowledge of the aircraft.'

He likened the difference between flex and fixed wing microlights as that between motor bikes and cars. 'Flexed wings give you a lovely style and flying in the open with the smell of the mountains and fold back wings for trailering. However, it is seasonal. Whereas fixed wings give you greater choice with more comfort and in my aircraft I can fly 500 miles at 100mph.'

When I told friends that I was soon to be going up in a microlight, weather conditions permitting, I was invariably met with the reply: 'You wouldn't catch me in one of those things. They look bloody dangerous.'

Although they didn't all swear of course, they all had the same image of a microlight — a big canvas wing with some kind of metal frame underneath to which was attached a lawn mower type engine making an awful noise.

That was my first impression, too, until I read up a bit about these machines and found they had developed quite a lot since their inception less than forty years ago. But when I arrived at Sabre Air Sports and was shown the Eurostar in which I would fly with Steve, my instructor, it really was an eye-opener. Like its namesake, it looked a real thorough-bred and very trendy. 'It's a day for sun glasses,' said Steve.

But first I had to get on board. To achieve this you had to climb up on to the wing, making sure you only put your feet on the walk-way, and then swing into the cockpit fitted with two snug seats side by side. After switching the engine on, Steve told me to pull the choke right out and then went through the panel instruments with me while waiting for the oil pressure to increase. With safety belts fastened, head-phones on and checking with the control tower, we were ready for take-off. Steve had the option of taking off from the grass but because it was muddy he chose the tarmac. Hardly making a sound, it sped along the ground and within seconds we were airborne and heading through a slight haze and up towards the clouds sitting on top of the valley.

'I think we'll head towards the Wye Valley,' said Steve. 'It'll be lovely above the clouds.' And so it proved. But first there were a few bumps under the fuselage and my stomach made a few turns. From below clouds look pretty ordinary, but going through them and above they take on much more dramatic shapes and forms. They now resembled moun-tains and ice-flows, absolutely marvellous. Once above them, the sky was a brilliant blue, making the contrast with the white of the clouds even greater. 'That's how I keep a suntan all the year round by keep coming up here,' said Steve.

'We've got to have visual contact with the ground,' Steve remarked, 'so we see where we're going by looking down through the holes in the clouds. If there weren't any holes we wouldn't be allowed up here and we'd have to fly below them.'

Through just such a hole I could see green fields, some of them covered with water, a reminder of recent downpours. Steve then showed me that with just a slight touch on the control stick the aircraft went either to the right or left.

'It's very sensitive,' I said.

'No, it's positive, but you touch it sensitively.'

With Hereford lying unseen to the left, we flew on at a cruising speed of 100 mph towards Hay, which we reached within 15 minutes of taking off. Not bad going, I thought. Now we veered over towards the Black Mountains, in sharp perspective and looking very bold and dramatic, especially the highest peak, Pen y Fan. Rising from them were a couple of gliders, newly airborne from Talgarth. Now the valley floor was empty of clouds which nestled on top of the mountain range, with shreds at the edges. As we got closer, so the turbulence grew and our flight was a bit bumpy. But as we climbed and veered to the left we were back over the clouds again.

'We speak of the freedom of the skies,' said Steve, 'but we've always got to remain vigilant.' So we both peered around before our next manoeuvre — depressing the aircraft nose up and down to decrease or increase speed. This was achieved by just pressing the joystick forward or backwards with finger or thumb. You could actually feel a slight resistance on the stick, and if you took your hand away, the aircraft would slowly right itself with the nose at the right angle. Again the importance of using the horizon as the correct position for the aircraft was emphasised by Steve.

'This is a very stable aircraft,' he added. 'It always comes back to its correct position. If you set the trim,' and here he had his hand on another lever positioned between the two seats, 'it will fly by itself. Then you can use both hands to look at maps or whatever.'

What a marvellous idea, I thought. You can let the plane fly by itself.

'And its very safe, too,' continued Steve. 'If the engine stalled' and he turned our speed down to its minimum 'from our height of 2,000ft we would have a radius of 20 square miles in which to land, and with its ability to land on grass over a very short distance, there would always be some suitable field to do this.' So that was reassuring as well.

Then he showed me how to turn the microlight. By putting the foot on the left floor pedal it swung sharply to the left, as if about to fall out of the sky. And vice-versa. It was indeed very manoeuvreable.

'A good little plane in which to do aerobatics,' I commented. 'Yes, except we are not allowed to. But in Czechoslovakia, where it was built, they do.' Looping the loop would be great fun, I mused.

*A flurry of flexwings for a Transport Day at Weston Park near Telford in the 1980s. (Neville Payne)*

Incredibly our time in the air was coming to an end and making our way back to Shobdon we flew past the water-filled fields behind which was a veritable sea, which turned out to be the controversial polytunnels under which strawberries are grown.

We veered round and then flew parallel with the airfield before making another turn at the end and beginning our descent. We came down at a steep angle and approached the tarmac at quite a speed but the landing was perfect, hardly a shudder or shake, and, again, within a very short distance we had landed.

'Very smooth,' I said.

'Well, I have done this a few times before,' said Steve.

'I mean the whole thing is very smooth. She's a great little plane.'

'One of the best.' We taxied over to the hangar, the weather now comparatively grey. It certainly didn't seem like an hour since we had taken off.

Steve's wife, Gerry, later told me that it takes about 45 hours to obtain one's National Private Pilot's Licence (NPPL), but it depends largely on the individual — their ability, commitment and how often they can come. It costs £95 an hour including another hour briefing and de-briefing. Written examinations have to be passed in such subjects as navigation, meteorology, air law and the principles of flight.

*An Alpha flexwing over Hereford in 1986. (Neville Payne)*

After learning to fly, one can take advantage of the club facilities including sales, servicing and social, with events such as fly-ins, barbecues, and weekend trips, even crossing the Channel to France and beyond.

Having experienced the top end of the microlight range, I now wanted to check out the flexwing machines with their more exposed, down to earth appeal. After various lines of enquiry I found myself driving through farmland on the outskirts of Hereford to Broad Meadow Farm and the Wye Valley Flyers. Here I met up with Neville Payne and other members in the clubhouse, a converted Portacabin soon to be replaced by a bigger, better one.

Neville is at 70 years of age the oldest member and has to have a doctor's declaration of fitness every six months. He explained that the club was started about 12 years ago since when a barn has been converted from agricultural use into a hangar where some 15 microlights are kept. Beyond is a 450 metre long grass airstrip, complete with windsock.

Before that he and another member, Brian Crockett, had started up a microlight centre at Haywood, a farm about a mile from Broad Meadow. They converted a wartime ammunition bunker, around which were big mounds of earth, into a hangar and opened an airstrip. It is still used today with about half a dozen machines using the hangar.

They both trained with John Hollins of Shobdon's Microflight in the 1980s, where everyone used to congregate. But the microlight flyers started to drift away as the school changed hands, coupled with the emergence of small clubs further south, together with cheaper hangarage. Now there is nowhere in the southern Marches where flexwing flying is actually taught. People have to travel to places like Long Marston, near Stratford-upon-Avon, or even Swansea and Haverfordwest.

'Flexwings are not easy to fly but they are good fun,' said Neville, who is on his sixth microlight after over 20 years of flying. 'It's more physical than being a stick-twiddler in the more modern machines.'

Fly-ins, barbecues and trips to various places in Europe are popular club events. For instance last year a group flew to Berlin and then to Switzerland, where microlights were being allowed to land for the first time.

The sound of the telephone ringing woke me from my slumbers early one March morning. 'Hello, it's Neville here. It's a lovely day for flying. Want to go up?'

'Why not,' I responded. I opened the curtains and the sun, which had been in short supply in the last few weeks, burst through. Definitely a great day to go up in a microlight, I thought.

I met up with Neville in the newly installed replacement Portacabin which serves as the clubhouse. Other members came and went, all offering a friendly word.

'I'll take you up myself,' he said. 'But you'll need to put on a flying suit.'

*Neville Payne in his Quasar microlight at the Wye Valley Flyers 'airfield'*

*Neville Payne with his hands on the control bar*

This appeared to be much too small to start with but after you've stepped into the legs and fastened them up there is a middle piece of cloth which fits over the chest and the whole thing fits quite snugly.

'You'll need this too,' and Neville passed over a Balaclava. 'It gets a bit chilly up there.'

We went out to the hangar, painted an environmentally friendly green, in front of which stood Neville's microlight, a Quasar, which cost £4,500, and has a two-stroke Rotax engine. To complete my kitting out, I had to put on a crash helmet with a visor and a head-phone. I really felt the part now. Getting into the tiny cockpit was a bit of a struggle, with my legs out wide and feet on pedals. I was then strapped in. The seat was comfy but the high head-rest forced my head forwards. Neville nonchalantly climbed in, sitting between my legs. Turning the intercom on, he asked: 'Everything okay. Ready for take-off?' With that, he turned the engine on, which, at the second attempt, sprang into life and we bumped over the grass to the runway, along which we taxied before turning round at the end.

*Neville, with young lady passenger, getting ready for take off in his Quasar at Broad Meadow in 2006. (Neville Payne)*

'With the two of us and a full tank of petrol, I'll have to give it full throttle,' he said. Which he duly did and we zoomed along the grass, before suddenly taking off and climbing steeply. I moved my head from side to side to get better views as the fields beneath us spread further and further out. Looking straight down, however, was a bit scary — there appeared to be nothing between me and the ground, a long way down.

'How do you like it?' queried Neville, as we reached a height of 1,400ft at a speed of 65mph. 'There's quite a strong head-wind.'

'It's fantastic.' It really was and although exposed to the elements, I felt nice and snug in my flying gear.

We followed the course of the meandering Wye, with Neville using the bar in front of him to steer the machine. 'Isn't that a bit tiring?' I asked.

'You get used to it, although flying this is pretty physical. But, if the conditions are right, you can always rest your arms.' We flew on along the valley leading to the Brecons before veering off and heading towards Weobley, with the church spire clearly visible and the school standing out with all its buildings and playing fields. Now flying at a height of 3,000ft we could see Dilwyn, my home village, before looking down on Leominster.

'See that long, straight road down there,' Neville said, pointing to a road by the industrial estate. 'That's where a light aircraft came down a few years back. Pilot thought he was landing at Shobdon.' Must have been a bit of a shock to any passing motorist, I thought. As we swung round, heading towards Hereford, I could see the dreaded polytunnels spreading like waves below, then the Cadbury factory and the distinctive outline of Dinmore Hill. Thermals were now hitting us and Neville grappled with the bar to keep the machine on an even course.

'Sorry its a bit bumpy,' he said as we went up and down a bit. I checked with my stomach — it was still there. We passed over watery gravel pits, flooded fields and the muddy River Lugg before reaching the outskirts of Hereford over which we flew. The Cathedral was almost lost amidst the surrounding buildings but the silver roofs of the new Asda supermarket sparkled and stood out.

'Height and speed equals safety,' said Neville as we came in to land. As we descended steeply another microlight was taking off forcing Neville to land from the other end, the one closest to a few houses. 'I hate landing this end,' he said, turning sharply to make the approach. We seemed to be heading for some bushes before Neville aborted the landing and we shot up again. After another sharp turn we came in at the other end, hitting the runway at speed before levelling out smoothly and pulling up. We taxied gently back to the hangar.

'How did you like it then?' queried Neville, disembarking.

'Absolutely brilliant,' I said. 'That's what I call proper flying.' Neville had to assist me out of the cockpit, both my legs having gone a bit dead. However, a few stamps and they seemed to be back to normal. As we walked over to the clubhouse, two microlights took off, one after the other, and were soon lost to sight.

Another member I spoke to was John Hunt, who has been flying since 1975 and has now logged up to 1,000 hours on hang gliders and 2,000 hours on microlights. Years ago he bought the first Soarmaster, designed and built in the United States, to be imported into this country and has flown all over south Wales and Devon and all round France and Spain. He bought the Soarmaster through Gerry Breen, who set up the Welsh Hang Gliding and Paragliding School in Abergavenny and now lives in Portugal. In 1979 Gerry set up a non-stop distance record for a foot-launched powered hang glider flying 202 miles to Norwich in about four hours. John recalled an incident at the Usk gliding club when Gerry put his foot through his hang glider's propeller and lost several toes. 'He was rushed away to hospital and I de-rigged his hang glider for him,' said John.

John has also designed and built microlights, the Huntwing, the plans for which he now sells, and is a senior inspector and check pilot. 'I enjoyed the old days when the sport was new and adventurous,' he added, 'and designing and building microlights. When I fly I don't hang around the fields, I like to do a lot of travelling.'

# Paragliding

Following the success of hang gliding (see the previous chapter), flying enthusiasts began looking at other ways of producing lightweight aircraft and thus opening up aviation to the masses, rather than being confined to an elite class. Some began looking at the possibilities of adapting the parachute and the first few pioneering paragliding flights were made during the 1960s and '70s in the French and Swiss Alps. Daredevils, taking pleasure in both the thrill of skydiving and jumping off cliffs, began experimenting by launching skydiving parachutes off steep mountain slopes and gliding down to the bottom. The first attempts were made with nothing more than a conventional parachute attached to the back of those jumping. But modifications were made with parachute designers coming up with more wing-like designs, and by 1978 the sport of paragliding was born in Mieussy, France. It soon spread to the UK with Neil Slinger one of the first people to paraglide here. With further development the possible angle of ascent increased from a 2:1 ratio to as high as 10:1 today.

Configuration of the wings is the main difference between hang gliding and paragliding. A hang glider's wings are V-shaped with a frame, while that of a paraglider is soft and more oval-shaped. Paragliders are also extremely portable: they fold up into a large rucksack which can be tossed into a car or on the back of a motorbike making the act of flying spontaneous.

A series of cords, known as risers, hang from the canopy or wing which are attached to the pilot's harness and from which he is suspended in a supine position. As the paraglider travels at much slower speeds than a hang glider, it is theoretically easier to fly. Although usually launched from a hill-top, they can also be released by the tow method in which an engine-driven winch pulls the machine into the air.

The introduction of specially designed engines has made paragliding even more versatile. Known as paramotoring, the pilot wears the engine on his back (like a rucksack) and this can provide thrust to take off literally anywhere. No more steep hills to climb. Then, once aloft, the paramotor can be used to motor along or soared in thermal lifts to make long cross-country runs. The motor, the simplest being a small two-stroke petrol engine, can be stopped and re-started using an electric starter. Thus the pilot has the freedom to enjoy either power-assisted flight or free flying depending on the weather conditions. Being foot launched there is no need of an airfield and easily de-rigged can be put in the boot of a car. Yet another recent development is the addition of a trike undercarriage with wheels.

One of the first free flight schools to be established in the country, certainly in this region, was the Welsh Hang Gliding and Paragliding School in Abergavenny. It was set up in 1975 by Gerry Breen to take advantage of some of the marvellous hill ranges in the area including Hay Bluff, Pandy, Blorenge, Merthyr and further to the east Rhossili Bay in the Gower near Swansea. After several changes of ownership and a change of name to Welsh Airsports, it has been owned for the past two years by Edi Geczy, who is also the chief instructor. It is based in a paraglider shop in Abergavenny which, according to Edi, is 'in the centre of the paragliding universe.' But to be closer to the M4, along which most of his customers drive, he is moving to new premises in Caerphilly. Twice as big as the old shop, there will be room to lay out the paraglider for instruction purposes and to carry out servicing. And Edi hopes to re-start hang gliding instruction which has languished in recent years. Edi also runs an apprentice instructor scheme, covering all aspects of flying, gaining the necessary qualifications, and the business/office work.

Edi can call on two or three other instructors to assist in running the courses conducted under British Hang Gliding and Paragliding Association (BHPA) and British Microlight Aircraft Association (BMAA) regulations. A variety of different training courses are offered to suit all tastes ranging from a one-day course costing £150, to the elementary pilot (EP) course with five or six days of tuition at a cost of £550, and a further course up to club pilot (CP) level costing £850. The complete course comprising both EP and CP can be obtained at the reduced price of £1,250. Cost of a new paraglider is about £2,500, although second hand ones are considerably cheaper. A harness, helmet, flight suit and boots will also be needed.

Because the weather plays such an important part in free flight, Edi also offers training courses abroad, particularly in Morocco where he is establishing a Welsh Airsports branch. Two weeks including air fare and accommodation on a B&B basis costs about £1,600. Edi also arranges paragliding holidays in France, Spain, Italy, Hungary and Nepal.

Edi's interest in aviation started at a young age, following in the footsteps of his father, a pilot in the Hungarian Air Force, who came to this country in 1956 after the Hungarian Revolution. His first flight was at the age of 12 in an old glider. He began taking lessons at 16 and after an interval got his licence at 25 and began doing aerobatics. He left the sport again until the age of 37 when he started to think how he could travel around Africa in some kind of flying machine. He saw a para-motor on TV and thought that was the perfect way. But it was not until a year later that he decided to take up paragliding seriously, become an instructor and leave his job as a DJ at a night club. He then spent two years as a civilian instructor at the Joint Services Hang Gliding Club at Crickhowell before buying Welsh Air Sports. In addition to teaching flying courses and running holidays abroad, Edi has also been involved in advertising projects, worked for TV including BBC Wales and Channel 4, and was once even asked to spread the ashes of a deceased person over their home village.

I had other plans for Easter Day but when Edi phoned the day before and said the weather was perfect for paragliding and would I like to go up, I could hardly refuse. Hadn't I been waiting weeks, no months, for the weather to improve? 'We're going to Rhossili. See you in the car park there at 10 o'clock.'

I must admit I was quite excited at the prospect of going up in a paraglider, probably the best way of experiencing flying as nature intended, but nervous at the same time. A paraglider seemed to be just a little on the frail side, that's all. But as it was to be my last flight, for the book that is, I hoped it would be a memorable one. Anyway, I left home the following day with, as Edi had directed, a packed lunch, bottle of water, boots, fleece and waterproof jacket. The weather looked just right — blue skies and sunshine.

I arrived an hour and a half late, but Edi and some of the trainees were still in the car park, converted farmer's fields already jam-packed with holiday makers. I climbed the hill with Edi, unmistakeable with 'Flying Instructor' on the back of his jacket, and a hat only half covering his long locks of pepper and salt hair.

'If you're not a pilot, why do you want to write this book?' he asked as we stopped for breath half way up. Good question. I then tried to explain that I thought a beginner's view on flying might be useful, and encourage more people to take up the sport.

Edi's students, all at different stages of the course, were waiting for us on the lower of the two hills overlooking Rhossili Bay, and what a staggering view. From the tapering Worms Head the bay curved round to its northernmost point at Burry Holms, with golden sands and way out the sea gently rolling in on white crested waves.

But to the matter at hand. Michelle Hall, Edi's assistant, was making ready her paraglider. She had unrolled the canopy, made from a special nylon, out on the ground and was now spreading the risers, or cords, into an orderly line. These were then gathered together at either end in bigger cords with rings attached, through which the pilot's hands are placed to direct and steer the glider. Along the top of the canopy was a series of air vents, reaching two-thirds of the way down, which fill with air. She then hitched on the harness, or portable armchair, containing a jelly bag or air pack provided as a safety measure but also for comfort if the landing is made on one's backside. As a matter of no particular interest, Brits always try to land on their feet, while the Italians apparently like to land on their bums. Also included in the harness is a reserve parachute — just in case.

Paragliding was no more difficult for women than for men, Michelle said, as it was more a question of technique than physical strength. After a two-day taster, she had been enjoying the sport for the last five years.

With the addition of a helmet and a two-way radio, she was ready to go. Meanwhile Edi, having briefed the trainees, had erected a windsock, bearing the Welsh dragon, to check wind direction. Everything was fine. Michelle, facing away from the sea, started to raise the canopy which began filling with air and, steadying it with the brake at the back of the canopy, executed a nifty about-turn and then ran, feet sometimes lifting off the ground, directly towards the edge of the hill-top. The canopy gently lifted her into the air and she was away.

110

*Preparing for take off at Rhossili*

One by one, the rest of the trainees prepared to get ready, only one being in the air at any one time so that Edi had direct contact with them all the time. They all seemed level-headed chaps with no desire to show off.

Mark Bowley, a security guard, explained that launching was the most difficult part, but once you were in the air 'it was awesome.' But at the moment he had to concentrate on his landings. He took off and after gliding along the hill ridge turned seawards and then back along the beach to his landing spot, a 20 yard circle drawn in the sand, guided in by Michelle. He made several tacks but overshot the mark before landing. Later, Mark returned to the hill-top, breathing heavily after the climb with an 18 kilo pack on his back. 'That's the worst part,' he panted.

Other members of the group took their turn in getting airborne. We were now joined by other paragliders, including several women, all bent on making the most of the beautiful weather. With the wind off the sea warmed up, it was now rising nicely as it hit the hills. Another 200ft higher up from us some more paragliders were lifting into the air. Soon there were a dozen machines in the air, together with a couple of hang gliders, all soaring and dancing gracefully in the sky. I stood entranced watching them, the variously coloured canopies making a splash of colour against the picture card blue sky, and couldn't wait for my turn to come around. However, I had to be patient as Edi wanted to get all his group airborne. 'Do you want to do some aerobatics?' Edi asked. 'Yes, please,' I responded, not knowing quite what I was letting myself in for. 'With this good lift coming off the ridge of the hill, we should be able

111

to stay up for half an hour or so. I'll let you take over the controls for a bit and you'll get a better idea of what it's like.' Couldn't be better, I thought.

Waiting to do his last flight before getting his club pilot certificate was Barry Adams, from Cambridge, who played rugby until he was 47 and was then looking for another sporting interest. After a long spell of indecision he eventually had his first flight on his 50th birthday, encouraged by his wife. Since then he had flown in Spain and Morocco.

'You are on your own up there,' he said. 'It is entirely up to you. You try and do everything Edi has told you on the ground. There is a big difference between paragliding and a team sport like rugby.' As a service engineer travelling around the country, Mark is now finding that paragliding is the ideal sport to fit into his work patterns.

Another of the group, Shane, who seemed addicted to adrenalin pumping sports including mountaineering and parachuting, was picking up the sport very quickly. He seemed a natural.

However, one of Edi's group, David Leake, was having a bit of a problem trying to take off. He was apparently unable to control the brake to keep the canopy in an upright position before turning around to make his run. The result was that he was being dragged about by the canopy, trampling over other people and their gear. Edi, who complained the trainee hadn't been practising enough, shouted 'bend your elbows.' It was to be his third or fourth attempt before at last he was airborne and doing well. By this time a mist was creeping in over the sea and creating quite a cloud over the hill-tops. Edi had already been up to investigate the wind situation and, at the same time, test a new design of canopy. He made it look all too easy, from effortless take-off to swinging the glider around, and coming into land on a small piece of grass between us. Edi advised David to keep away from the ridge and he glided towards the sea. 'Peachy,' Edi said. 'Now try doing a Big Ears,' he instructed over the radio. And David lowered the tips of the canopy, arresting his descent. There was not enough lift for him to come back to our hill so he eventually landed on the beach.

Mark Bowley again re-appeared after climbing back up the hill. 'At least I'm consistent,' he said. 'I landed on the same spot as I did before!'

With the sea mist appearing to be less thick, Edi decided it was time to take me up, over six hours after I'd first arrived. Not that I was

*Airborne*

complaining. It was fascinating just watching all the activity in such glorious surroundings. Strapped into the harness which covered my bottom, I now found it difficult to walk let alone run. However Michelle and another trainee steadied the reins, and Edi, who was strapped on behind me, raised the canopy. We turned around and I was instructed to run which I did like a drunken crab. We came to a halt and then started running again, the edge of the hill getting closer and closer. I stumbled and my knees were protruding as we skimmed the ground and then bang, my right knee smacked against a rock, disguised by grass, as we took off at speed. Looking down I could see a big rip in my trouser leg. I was told to free my arms from the harness. We kept going and were then skimming along the side of the hill, breathtakingly close. This is the trouble flying tandem — you are in the front but have no control. To say I wasn't a little scared would be an under-statement. We turned and Edi tried to gain height. Amongst the bracken below were sheep, including one that looked decidedly dead. 'I'm not getting much lift,' Edi shouted. 'I'll have to land on the beach. Put your hands through the harness again.' We slowly descended and landed gently on the sand. My knees immediately buckled and I was scrabbling in the sand with the canopy wanting to take off again before Edi unharnessed me. I looked at my knee through the slit and noticed a lot of blood.

'You're the first person I've injured doing this,' said Edi, looking concerned, as I tied a handkerchief round my knee.

'Not to worry,' I said. 'It wasn't your fault. I was just clumsy.' I didn't like telling him that I was rather accident prone.

'Strange about the wind,' he said. 'It just seemed to peter out.' I suppose we had been airborne for less than five minutes, and I hadn't even looked up to see the billowing canopy.

It would have been nice to have gone for a swim, but the sea — although the tide was coming in — was still miles out. With Edi carrying the canopy and me the harness we trudged back up the hillside, stopping frequently for me to get my breath back. We re-joined the others on the hill-top, some preparing to leave, and were told that other paragliders taking off just after us experienced the same problem with the air just dying out. One glider had come down on the hillside, its canopy looking like, well, a dead sheep.

While we waited to see if the sea mist would lift, Edi put a dressing on my knee and then after another trainee, Simon, an air traffic controller at Bristol airport, had put in a call to check the weather, we decided to call it a day. Escorted by a solicitous Michelle, I joined the others in the car park, where all the paragliders, in their rucksacks, were stowed in the back of Edi's car. Then we moved on to the Worms pub, lively with outdoor enthusiasts seeking refreshment. After a couple of beers and a chat, I decided it was time to start the long drive home. Edi's last words were: 'Perhaps you'd like to have another flight tomorrow. We'll probably be taking off somewhere near Newport.'

I made my excuses. Apart from the fact that by now my knee was swelling up and hurting, I felt that discretion was the better part of valour. It was a great shame as I hadn't really enjoyed my experience. I would loved to have been up in the sky soaring with the birds. Unfortunately, this was not to be. But I sincerely hope my experience does not put anyone off.

For Edi, he is now nearer to fulfilling his dream of flying around Africa. Next year he hopes to cross the Sahara desert from north to south in a paramotor with one or two other enthusiasts. 'If we fly with the wind behind us, we can achieve a ground speed of 50mph and cover about 100 miles in a day,' he said enthusiastically. A film company involved with the BBC is interested in covering the trip. If the journey is successful, he then hopes to fly from London to Cape Town. I'm sure it will be the trip of a life-time, but I for one won't be volunteering.

# Home Built Aircraft

Some people are not only interested in aviation and flying, but in building their own aircraft and tinkering about with engines. To meet this growing demand, a range of light aircraft and microlights are available in kit form, usually from the USA, often with 'quick-build' options, or from a set of plans. For the more adventurous there is also the possibility of making an aircraft to one's very own design. In addition to licensed airfields, there are a number of private airstrips from where the aircraft can be flown providing permission has been obtained. These are mainly grass airstrips on farmers' land with adjacent hangars. There are a dozen or so in this area ranging from Milson, near Clee Hill in Shropshire to Painscastle in Radnorshire, and 2,000 in the UK as a whole.

The umbrella organisation covering recreational aviation and amateur aircraft builders is the PFA, or Popular Flying Association, which gives considerable help to anyone building their own aircraft.

After a new project has been registered, experts from the PFA's engineering department carry out numerous inspections as the construction work proceeds. On completion, test flights are carried out before a Permit to Fly can be issued. Unlike a Certificate of Airworthiness, this has certain restrictions: daytime flying only, no flying over built-up areas, no 'right of flight' outside the UK, and for private, recreational use only. The permit is renewed annually, rather like a car's MOT, when the aircraft is again inspected. With plane building taking up to ten years for some people, PFA inspectors find themselves giving not only advice but psychological support as well.

The cost of building an aircraft varies enormously from about £5,000 for a single-seater microlight such as a Mini-Max, to over £50,000.

The PFA also offers a National Private Pilot's Licence (NPPL), which has both advantages and limitations. To start with, the course is less complex and onerous than the Private Pilot's Licence (PPL) and takes about a dozen hours less flying time; 22 hours with an instructor and 10 hours solo is the minimum. Then there are navigation and flying skill tests and a series of ground examinations. Limitations include day flying and not in clouds, only in the UK, and with a maximum of four people, including the pilot. Other advantages are that only a doctor's certificate of fitness is needed and not a full medical, and that pilots of different types of aircraft get a credit for that experience if they want to fly another type of aircraft.

The Popular Flying Association has a number of branches called struts which provide the focus for local members. One such is Shobdon Strut, based at the Herefordshire Aero Club clubhouse, whose co-ordinator is David Johnstone. He explained that the Strut was a self-help organisation, and held regular meetings often with guest speakers. For instance, the speaker in May 2007 was Manuel Querioz, the naturalised Portuguese from the Vale of Evesham, who the previous year became the first Briton to fly around the world in a home built aircraft. Then there are visits to places of aviation interest and an annual fly-in at Shobdon.

David is himself in the process of constructing a home built aircraft. He is part of a six-man syndicate which hopes during 2007 to complete an American designed two-seater RV9A after two to three years of work at a cost of about £50,000. The plane will have a top speed of 160mph and will be able to travel for an hour on 15 litres of jet fuel, or in other words, fly about 160 miles for £7.

Another aviator who has built his own aircraft is David Corbett, company secretary and retired director of Corbett Farms Ltd., now run by his son Richard, owners of Shobdon airfield. He took six years, from 1996 to 2001, to build a two-seater Europa, from a kit designed by the British aircraft designer, Ivan Shaw, with a range of between 450 and 500 nautical miles and a cruising speed of 110 nautical miles an hour. David, who first started flying light aircraft at Shobdon in 1963, soon hopes to have flown his Europa to every country on the Continent. He has been a member of the PFA for 12 years.

What advice would he give to anyone thinking of building their own aircraft? 'Don't be frightened. If I can do it, anyone can. You will get an enormous amount of fun in both building and flying it.'

# Bibliography

Brew, Alec and Barry Abraham *Images of Aviation — Shropshire Airfields*

Brooks, Robin J. *Herefordshire and Worcestershire Airfields in the Second World War* (2006)

Bruce, Gordon *Charlie Rolls — pioneer aviator* (1990)

Druce, Fred *Remembrance of Things Past — Ross-on-Wye*

Grant, Mike and Derrick Pratt *Wings Across the Border — A History of Aviation in North Wales and the Northern Marches*

Hales, Brian *Eardisley Characters and Capers*

Hughes, Philip *Wings Over The Wye* (1984)

Langland, Stephen *Gliding from Passenger to Pilot* (2001)

Macklin, Fiona, *The Story of RAF Madley* (2006)

McKaig, W.H. *Early Photographs of Radnor*

Moore, L.P. *A Synoptic History of the Midland Gliding Club* (1964)

Neal, Toby *Shropshire Airfields* (2005)

Pfuell, Ivor *A History of Shobdon* (1994)

Prescott, Colin *To the Edge of Space (Adventures of a Balloonist)* (2000)

Rennison, John *Wings over Gloucestershire* (2000)

Rolt, L.T.C. *A History of Ballooning* (1966)

Sandford, Anne *Hereford and Herefordshire in Old Photographs*

Waters, Gwen *The Story of Churchdown* (1999)

Whitehead, David *Hereford*


Newspapers and Magazines:
*Berrow's Worcester Journal*
*Gloucester Journal*
*Hereford Journal*
*Hereford Citizen and Bulletin*
*Hereford Times*
*Monmouthshire Beacon*
*Motorsport*
*Radnor Express*
*Ross Gazette*
*Shropshire Star*
*The Aeroplane*
*Whitchurch Herald*

# Index